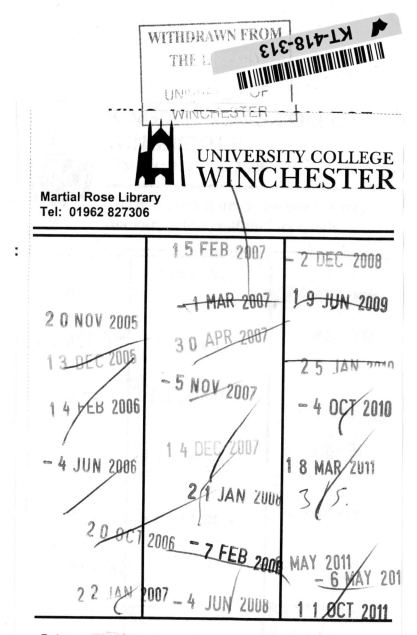

UNIVERSITY COLLEGE
WINCHESTER

Martial Rose Library
Tel: 01962 827306

To be returned on or before the day marked above, subject to recall.

Meriwether Publishing Ltd., Publisher
Box 7710
Colorado Springs, CO 80933

Editor: Arthur Zapel
Typesetting: Sharon Garlock
Cover design: K. Anne Kircher

© Copyright MCMLXXXVIII Meriwether Publishing Ltd.
Printed in the United States of America
First Edition

Library of Congress Cataloging-in-Publication Data

Keller, Betty.
　　Improvisations in creative drama.

　　Summary: Provides workshop activities and dramatic sketches for student actors.
　　1. Drama in education.　2. Children's plays, American.　[1. Improvisation.　2. Acting.　3. Plays]
I. Title.
PN3171.K34　1988　　　371.3'32　　　88-60079
ISBN 0-916260-51-8

4　5　6　7　8　9　　　99　98　97　96　95

This book is dedicated to a group of exceptional young actors with whom I have worked: Angi, Arleigh, Becki, Jade, Jane, Kim, Linda, Lona, Marilyn and Patti. BRIDGEWORK is especially dedicated to my son, Christopher, and IN THE MIDDLE OF THE NIGHT to my son, Perry. For his helpful criticism, a special thanks to Jake Zilber.

TABLE OF CONTENTS

Part I: CREATIVE DRAMA WORKSHOPS

Part II: DRAMATIC SKETCHES

APPENDIX:

Part I

CREATIVE DRAMA WORKSHOPS

AUTHOR'S NOTE

Section one of this book describes only the beginning of a long process. Although some of the activities it suggests may appear frivolous on the surface, they conceal a deeper purpose: to lure the student into an addiction to drama and theatre on a serious level.

The first section of this book is composed of an ordered sequence of workshops in Creative Drama, introduced by a few words on the mechanics of classroom management and student preparation. The theoretical approach and justification for Creative Drama I leave to authorities on the subject.

Each workshop is explained in detail as I have used it with my own students, but the form will change for each teacher. I have written it as if all students were thirteen years of age and reasonably intelligent, but I have used the same techniques with little modification when teaching seven-year-olds and when working with adults. A particular workshop may take twenty minutes, or it may involve students in a two- or three-hour session. In general, the more sophisticated the students, the more time will be required on each workshop. It's the degree of involvement that sets the limits.

If you explore every one of the activities suggested here, allowing sufficient time for development of the students' own creative extensions of them, you will have enough material for a year's work in the classroom. (That is, given the normal time allotment of three to four lesson-hours per week common in secondary schools.) However, the purpose of this material is not to supply you with lesson plans which will require slavish conformity. The title of it indicates the intent; the activities here are a point of departure, suggestions from which you are invited to take off.

PREPARATIONS

I. Before the Students Arrive

In the average public school the facilities provided for teaching conventional drama are usually somewhat makeshift, while the facilities for creative drama are almost non-existent. Both are subjects which most school officials did not anticipate and therefore did not provide for in school buildings. However, once the need for creative drama in the school has been recognized, the facilities are more easily available and much less expensive than those for conventional drama and acting classes. For one thing, no stage or auditorium is required; for another, costly scenery and costumes are unnecessary.

Then what exactly are the facilities that the creative drama teacher must have?

1. An empty room.

The usual classroom is stuffed with assorted educational furniture which should be eliminated. If other subjects must be taught in this room, have desks replaced by tables and chairs. They're easier to stack and are sometimes quite useful as mountains and ships' bridges. But if possible, dispose of all furniture except for a few sturdy tables, and a chair or stool for each student's use.

2. Basic drama room furniture.

The following items are extremely useful for imaginative

improvisations and for efficient classroom procedures:

    a) a number of small platforms, preferably four by four, a size easily manipulated by students, and economical where plywood comes in four by eight foot sheets;

    b) a number of sturdy wooden boxes of various sizes and shapes;

    c) a couple of short portable flights of stairs, three or four steps each and about three feet wide.

3. Sources of controllable light.

Ideally, these will be a number of spotlights mounted on movable stands, individually controlled by rheostats. But probably you'll be lucky to get half a dozen flashlights. A supply of colored theatrical gelatines is needed but even colored gift-wrapping cellophane will do in a pinch.

4. A tape-recorder and a record player.

For some of the lessons, it is very useful to have access to a number of portable cassette recorders as well.

5. Adequate storage space.

This should include some cupboards which lock for storing more valuable equipment such as records and players, and bins for collections of small properties. My most useful storage items are three wooden bins two feet by two feet by three feet deep mounted on heavy-duty casters that I can move out to the center of the room during classes.

6. Inspirational equipment.

These are the supplies that are usually unavailable on school board order forms and must be painstakingly collected:

    a) music on records and tapes. It is an almost constant chore to collect music which will inspire drama. Tape anything you hear that might be useful at a later date. Listen for electronic music, jazz, symphonies, movie music tracks, and sound effects. Modern pop songs are usually useless for promoting imaginative responses;

    b) reproductions of art works. Your school librarian will know where to find these in books and in magazines; indeed she might even start a clippings file for you!

    c) large photos of interesting faces and places, preferably

in color;

d) a collection of junk. Never throw anything away unless it smells unbearably! Save old clothing (especially hats and accessories), sea shells, odd-shaped containers, old jewelry, eyeglasses, interesting fabrics and bits of fur, chunks of metal, wood, and plastic, pieces of dismembered engines and furniture, discarded dishes, umbrellas, toy guns, broken tools, seedpods and dried grasses, dolls, balls, rope, buckets, and ribbons. Sort them all into large containers stored where you can produce them at a moment's notice.

And what are the qualities that the teacher of creative drama must have?

I think there is just one essential. Patience!

When *creation* doesn't happen in the first week of workshops, relax! Be patient with imaginations that have been a long time unexercised. It usually takes six workshops with a new group before anything at all happens, and much longer than that before anything wonderful happens!

When the students are devising their improvisations, have the patience not to interfere just because the drama is not developing as you would have shaped it yourself. The urge to direct a drama can be almost overwhelming, but if the teacher can remain neutral, the end product often is more beautiful than anything the teacher could have achieved by meddling. Sometimes, of course, the moment is missed and the action turns aimless; one word of instruction could have corrected this but the joy of creation would have been partially destroyed. You'll have to learn when to help and when to remain silent.

When discussions are held, have patience to hear everyone's ideas, *really* hear them.

When the din becomes unbearable, have patience. Decide which of it is necessary for creation, and then caution the unnecessarily noisy groups individually. Don't impose blanket silence on group activity, unless you have a darn good reason. Kids working in groups, exchanging ideas, and planning actions are not quiet.

II. Preparing the Students

Setting a few basic rules at the beginning of the school year will make the rest of the year more enjoyable for teacher and students.

Prescribe the dress required in the drama room and insist that this be maintained. Sensible clothing includes:
> jeans or shorts or tights
> sweat-shirts or T-shirts
> running shoes or bare feet

Sometimes I ask my classes to bring an old shirt (one of father's will do) and to spend one or two classes decorating their "drama shirts" with lines from plays, cartoons of their favorite television characters, or masks of tragedy and comedy. These shirts can then be worn as smocks over other clothes. The object, of course, is to encourage clothing that allows mobility and is inexpensive.

Remind the students not to carry sharp objects in their pockets.

Classroom activities operate more smoothly if behavior limits are known. These are the basic ones that I have found useful:

Group work involves cooperation and compromise; there is not room in creative drama for those who must always have their own way. Students mustn't always expect to work with their close friends but must be prepared to work with everyone in the class.

Students must not interfere with the concentration of others by distracting them physically or in more subtle ways.

No one in creative drama "just watches". Everyone must be involved or an enforced division into actors and audience results. Since creative drama is intended to overcome the inhibitions many people feel in communicating, uninvolved watchers will defeat the whole program.

During discussions, all criticisms of the work of others must be constructive. Sometimes, small factions in the class will attempt to ridicule the efforts of others, gradually decreasing the creativity level of the class. When this happens, effective control has been taken from the teacher; but the real losers are the students themselves.

At the point in the school year when "audience" type activities are introduced, I invoke the rule of "No Defense to Criticism." Players are required to listen in silence while others explain what they "read" or understood in the presentation.

As the whole point of the presentation is to communicate, failure to communicate must be taken at face value. (In the same manner, a professional actor's performance must stand on its own merits when the curtain comes down.) This rule, incidentally, prevents most of the accusations and counter-accusations players like to indulge in when they are criticized.

> *"I didn't understand what John was supposed to be doing!"*
> *"Well, why didn't you watch me, stupid!"*

Combat and violence in improvisations must be kept under control for the sake of safety. Try instituting the "No Contact" method early in the year. (See Part One, Workshop 8)

Finally, I usually warn students early on the unnecessary use of offensive or overly suggestive ideas in improvisations. The easiest way to define such material is "things which might embarrass some members of the class". Young people commonly go through stages in which they produce what I call "toilet-bowl drama". They seem to believe that the only amusing material for improvisation is based on bodily functions. Usually one of these scenes touches off a whole rash of them. Depending on the class's maturity, I either specifically outlaw these dramas early in the year, or wait until a few have been presented and then hold a discussion. Very occasionally, neither has been necessary; student censure has done the job.

Chapter One

"NO AUDIENCE" ACTIVITIES

These activities are designed so that all class members participate simultaneously. There is no student preparation or rehearsal time; work is spontaneous.

In later chapters, workshops will be described that involve "performance", presentation by one group before the rest of the class, which functions as the "audience". This section involves no "performance" in that sense, and therefore no "audience"; as a result, these lessons are good starters.

Workshop 1: Painting with Music

Phase 1:

Select passages of music that give a variety of rhythms or moods (see Appendix). Have your students lie down on the floor with their arms extended beyond their heads. Explain that each one is now lying within a box whose ends may be just touched if the occupant stretches himself even more fully. By stretching his arms and legs to the sides, he may touch the side walls of the box. If he sits up and raises his arms above his head, he will be able to touch the ceiling of his box. He has ample room to move but not to stand up in his assigned space. Ask the students to examine the walls of their new homes, exploring the corners, feeling the textures. Reassure them that there will always be adequate light and air.

Now the music is played. The students begin with closed eyes. Suggest to them that they will find beside them one large pot of paint and all the painting equipment they desire. The paint is of a single color, and they are to let the "color" of the music determine it. They are to cover the entire inner surface of their boxes with it before the music runs out. Give the signal to open the eyes, remind them to paint into the corners and to paint the entire floor. No need to suggest that they keep time to the music; this is an automatic response.

When the music ends, it is time for a long quiet look at the colors produced.

Phase 2:

Now ask them to imagine that this colored box is their own secret hideout for the rest of their lives. This is to be their own personal private environment, completely independent of the rest of the world. Ask them to decide what additions of color and design they would make to provide their lives with variety and inspiration. Next, play a second musical selection; this time, whenever they think of a color, it will appear as a pot of paint beside them. If they allow themselves to think of another color, the first will disappear and be replaced by the new thought-color. They can decorate their boxes with as many colors as they choose, but they must concentrate carefully to get the desired results. The music itself will seem to force certain colors and designs, so they may have to concentrate hard whenever they want to counteract its influence.

When the music has finished, ask the students again to evaluate their hideouts (boxes). One panel of their boxes is removable; if they choose they may leave their boxes and look at them from the outside. If they wish, they may share their creation by "showing" it to someone else.

Now the boxes must be cleared away; students may move them to a position beside the door if they wish to keep them, or they may break them up and throw the pieces out of the window.

Discussion: What colors did you use? What designs? Why? Did the music control the colors? The design? Did your imagination overrule the music? Why did you destroy your box? Why do you want to keep it? Were you aware of the others? Have you ever been able to choose the decoration for a room? What decided the colors then? The design?

Variation 1:

Instead of boxes, have your students conjure up large clear

plastic balls or bubbles whose dimensions are determined by the occupant's reach. These have the disadvantage of allowing the occupant to stand while working, so that he may not discover the possibilities offered by other body positions. But if the classroom floor is not very clean, the advantages are obvious.

Variation 2:

Have students "blow" color onto the surfaces, big puffs for dark or strong colors, gentle breaths for pastel shades. They can then spread the colors with hands, fingers, elbows and feet.

Phase 3:

Select a whimsical piece of music (see Appendix) — for example, harpsichord music. Ask your students to close their eyes, opening them only when their imaginations have established shapes and colors. Before beginning the music, explain that they will find a very small intricate porcelain or clay statue beside them, small enough to fit into the palm of the hand. Beside it are a selection of colored glazes which must be applied to it to complete it. Ask them to begin when they can "see" it. Play the music. When the music ends, ask them to share their work with others, discussing and comparing.

Phase 4:

Select a vigorous march or similar piece of music (see Appendix). Divide the class into groups of four or five members. Explain to each group that a section of wooden fence, twelve feet long and ten feet high, stands before it. The group is to paint it front and back, top edge and bottom edge, within the time span of the music. Without any words being spoken or mouthed, the group must establish the fence's dimensions, find the necessary supplies, and help each other to complete the assignment.

Discussion: What color paint was used? Did all members of the group see it as the same color? What type of wood was used in the fence construction? What equipment was used? What proved to be the most effective means of communication? Did the music set the color? Slow down the pace of the workers? Speed it up? How many times did group members walk through the fence?

Variation 1:

Change the fence to a garage or shed. Specify the number of doors and windows.

Variation 2:

One member of each team becomes an inspector, inspecting not his own team's work but that of a rival one, checking that it doesn't miss any spots on the paint job, and that its members don't walk through their fence. Rather noisy, but fun.

Variation 3:

Assign the building of a fence or shed by team work, carefully specifying the number of boards to be used and the exact number of nails to be used per board. Again no verbal communication between team members is allowed. The inspector variation works well with this one.

Variation 4:

Assign one team at a time the task of constructing a shed or fence, the other teams drawing a picture of the shed they see being erected. The drawings may be done on the blackboard or on paper. The former method, of course, allows the performing team to learn how much they are communicating as they progress.

Workshop 2: Hand Plays

Phase 1:

Ask students to lie on the floor, raising their hands before their faces where they can examine them carefully. (It's important that they be lying down because this prevents them from watching what others are doing.) Ask them to imagine that this is the first time they have ever seen a hand. Have them turn it and contort it so that all its peculiarities may be studied. Introduce the idea that the hands have individual personalities independent of each other and of the body that claims them, and that each hand can represent an individual character as if each person had a pair of built-in puppets.

Now dictate a brief drama between an assured, determined right-hand character, and an awkward, reticent left-hand character. Each student works out the drama with his hands as the plot unwinds: the characters meet, they disagree, and right is victorious. New drama: right becomes a bully, left a little frail gentleman, but somehow the latter is victorious. Or suggest an encounter between two animals, perhaps a rabbit and a dog, or a squirrel and a hawk.

Next, select some music which has numerous mood variations and preferably two dominant solo instruments or two alternating themes (see Appendix). Plan a two-character plot which will follow the moods of the music, and quietly outline the plot as the music progresses. Each student works it out with his own hands. One precaution here: the plot should be predominantly physical, and slapstick humor seems to work the best.

Finally, select new music, suggest only the beginning of a plot, and let the students work out their own conclusions.

Once their imaginations are in high gear, they might enjoy evolving a plot from curtain to curtain.

Phase 2:

Have each student find a partner. The two then seat themselves facing one another. Partner A begins a hand play, Partner B being allowed to watch only the hands of the player. (The face of the player will be a dead giveaway.) Partner B must signal with his hands whenever he does not understand. Try fairy tales first, and then launch them on their own creations. Next reverse the roles so that Partner B has a chance to tell a story.

Phase 3:

Use the same technique with music as the inspiration, with first A, then B, taking over the interpretation of the music "plot".

Workshop 3: Sculpture with Invisible Clay

Phase 1:

Choose rich music that has a certain sweeping grandeur (see Appendix). The students' assignment is to create a piece of sculpture as the music dictates. All the clay that they require will appear beside them as they will it to appear. They must concentrate fully to see the work emerge from the clay. The size of the works will depend on the "size" of the music chosen.

Discuss the works created and the titles that the sculptors might give them.

Phase 2:

Partners. Two sculptors work together without spoken communication to produce a masterpiece. Time limit: the length of the chosen music. Each must name the work according to his own image of it.

Workshop 4: Sculpture with People Clay

This involves body contact without making a "big thing" of it.

Phase 1:

One partner arranges the other in a statue-pose, and names the "masterpiece" he has created. A show of all the statues created by the class follows, with prizes for the most imaginative, the most comic, the most likely to be exhibited in the National Gallery.

Phase 2:

Groups of three or four persons. One is the sculptor, the others are the clay. The sculptor is to combine all the clay and transform it into one large non-human sculpture. It is to be named and put on display for an auction attended by art lovers (that is, all the other sculptors) and sold to the highest bidder.

In Workshop 4, the rule "Be kind to your clay!" must be insisted upon in advance, because the sculptor becomes part of the clay next time. This rule will prevent bloodshed, should the over-eager sculptor be inclined to rough methods.

The sculptures may be timed by music, which may also help to set the mood. Or a simple clock-time may be set for completion of the work.

Workshop 5: The Prisoner

This lesson is based on the same urge that compels people

to watch horror shows and makes small children shiver with delight when the witch appears in Snow White.

Choose music that suggests dungeons and chains, and that builds to a good thunderous climax (see Appendix). The students are asked to lie on their backs on the floor. Explain that they awake from sleep to find themselves alone, imprisoned and chained by a wicked monster (or magician, or giant, or secret police chief) in the dungeon beneath an ancient castle. They are imprisoned there because they stole the monster's jewels (or the plans for a nuclear airplane, or the minutes of a secret oil-dealers' meeting in Afghanistan). Describe the clamps which fasten their ankles and wrists to the floor, secured there by great iron spikes pounded into the stone. Invite them to pull against the clamps as they wake from their sleep.

Begin the music. Whenever changes in the music allow for it, introduce new horrors to the chamber . . . water that runs across the floor so that the body has to be raised, a spider creeping over the hand, a fly buzzing and alighting. Toward the climax of the music introduce the footsteps of the approaching executioner, a mighty effort to break the clamps (an earthquake, if the music can manage it, will nicely facilitate this), and a dramatic escape at the eleventh hour.

Discussion: What sensations were the worst? What did you fear most in the dungeon? Did you see the executioner? What did he look like? What was the wicked monster like?

Variation 1: Tunnels

This has the same general plan but a tunnel of horrors is substituted for the dungeon, and the students are involved in much more physical activity. The students are chased through tunnels of various heights and widths, having to crawl through slimey passages, being lost in icy caves, climbing treacherous chimney-like openings, always just breaths away from discovery and capture by the villain.

Variation 2: Factory

The same plan as "The Prisoner" but the setting is a factory where huge machines become animated with malevolent intent. There is no escape from the factory and play only ceases when the machines run out of fuel (music), and return to their proper places in the imagination.

Workshop 6: Mirrors and Shadows

These old standbys for encouraging concentration have many interesting variations.

In *Mirrors,* students pair off facing one another. A begins a simple slow action with one hand, B duplicating this action as though he were the mirror-image of A. Therefore, if A is moving his right hand, B, facing him, will be moving his left hand.

Once the principle of the exercise is understood, the initiator of the action may broaden the area of movement, adding leg, head and torso movement. It will become increasingly difficult for the mirror-image to duplicate his partner's motions, as he can't watch all parts of the anatomy at once. At this point, suggest that he concentrate on his partner's eyes: he will learn what all actors know — that the eyes will give him most of the message.

The object, of course, is to work in harmony with a partner, not to trick him with fancy footwork or sudden moves.

In *Shadows,* the initiator of the action has his back to his partner, who must duplicate the action as though he were a shadow. The point of his concentration is the back of his partner's head, so the task is much more difficult. This exercise is not the same as the game of follow-the-leader, as here the intent, as in *Mirrors,* is to have the action of both partners occur at the same instant, almost as if the muscles in the initiator's body are raising and lowering the limbs of both initiator and duplicator.

In both *Mirrors* and *Shadows,* music is most helpful in setting the pace of movement.

Variation 1: Delayed-action Mirrors

In this form of *Mirrors,* the mirror-image duplicates the action only after it is complete. For this purpose, a complete action is designated as a body movement in a single direction. If a hand is raised it is a single action but it becomes a second action when the hand begins to move laterally. However, if the hand is raised and moved laterally *as it is raised,* it is a single action. A circular action (for example, moving the hand in a circle) is considered for this purpose to be a single action until it meets the point where it began.

Phase 1:

The initiator makes a single action. This may be with more than one part of the body as long as each body part makes a single action simultaneously. The mirror-image duplicates the action. The initiator makes a new action and the duplicator follows. They continue in this manner.

Phase 2:

The initiator is now given the right to make two consecutive actions before the mirror-image follows suit. In time, the initiator will be able to make six or seven consecutive actions without confusing his partner. Concentration and close observation during such a sequence are absolutely essential.

Phase 3:

Add sound effects to the actions. Decree that on the second and fifth action, for example, the initiator shall supply a sound effect to accompany that phase of the action. Now the initiator's task is as difficult as the duplicator's, trying to keep the series of actions and sounds correct.

Variation 2: Distorted Mirrors

In this variation, the mirror-image distorts the actions of the initiator, making them larger, or taller, or wildly misshappen. This can be done with both simple mirrors or delayed action mirrors.

Variation 3: Group Mirrors

One initiator is faced with a barrage of mirror-images.

All of these variations are easily adapted to exercises in *Shadows*, which is sometimes preferable when the class is unusually high-spirited.

Workshop 7: Machines

This activity is commonly used for investigating rhythm.

Phase 1:

Use a selection of music with a regular, unmistakeable beat (see Appendix). Each student, in a seated position, begins moving a leg or arm or head to the beat of the music, concentrating on establishing a distinctive pattern of action. For example, an arm is bent at the elbow with the fist at shoulder height, the fist is propelled forward straightening the arm, the fist returns to shoulder position bending the arm, the fist is propelled skyward straightening the arm, and then the fist is returned to its original position. This series of moves is repeated to become the pattern of action.

Next, the student begins to move another arm or leg so that somewhere in its pattern of action it will connect with the first pattern briefly, like the interconnection of two parts of a machine. It takes enormous concentration now to introduce a third pattern of action into this. It's rather like the old game of "Rub-your-tummy-and-pat-your-head". Thus his left knee, rising and falling, may thrust up the left arm which is making circular motions in front of the body striking the right elbow as it returns in its piston-like motion! The individual has now become a complicated machine, its impetus coming from the left leg . . . which is electrically energized by the music!

Phase 2:

Divide the class members into pairs. Each individual machine combines its moving parts with those of another, joining some parts securely (for example, locked hands or elbows), and interconnecting other parts so that they cause each other to move (for example, one's raised knee strikes the other's arm which causes it to collide with a head which then bumps . . . etc.). Finally the machine adds its own sound effects. The result is a human Rube Goldberg invention.

Phase 3:

Divide into groups of five or six persons. Assign the task of imitating the mechanism of a specific well-known appliance such as a toaster or a mixmaster. All persons in the group must represent moving parts. Have a competition to present "the most original imitation"!

Phase 4:

Assign the task of inventing a machine which the whole

world is waiting for, such as an automatic bed-maker, or a homework preparer.

Phase 5:

Spontaneous group machines. One player begins a pattern of action accompanied by a sound effect. Each new player may join the machine wherever he can add an inter-connecting part or complimentary action and a suitable sound effect. Finally all the class members should have become involved.

Variations:

The machine can break down when a part fails to operate properly, and "mechanics" may be assigned to repair it, either by getting the faulty part working again, or by substituting new parts.

Breakdown may also be done progressively, where a part breaks down but repairs itself as soon as another part collapses.

Workshop 8: Combat

There is always some danger of injury during classroom improvisations that involve physical encounters. If a non-violent technique is established early, this can be prevented. I've found this "no-contact" method to be very useful and to be an enjoyable experience in itself.

Music is used to establish a working rhythm; it should be slow, and waltz-like (see Appendix).

Phase 1:

Each student works by himself, attacking an invisible opponent who is determinedly counter-attacking. The student must concentrate to "see" the opponent and parry his blows. All the blows are to be in slow-motion to the rhythm of the music, carefully calculating the thrust and balance, and reacting to the blows "felt" as his opponent strikes back. When the students understand the slow-motion technique and the idea of reacting to blows and varying their counter-attacks, continue to Phase 2.

Phase 2:

Students work in pairs, this time attacking each other,

but never quite making contact. Use music again to reinforce the slow-motion edict. You can discuss with your students the fights they see in their favorite television shows where fancy feints and footwork add excitement (but little reality!) to the hero's hairbreadth escapes.

Sometimes, with more energetic classes, I require that the players remain on their knees until they have learned the rules. If a blow does connect in this position it has less force than one delivered in a standing position, and there is less distance for the victim to fall down.

Phase 3:

Introduce imaginary weapons such as fencing foils or broadswords to encourage better footwork.

Workshop 9: Instructing

This activity involves the student in instructing someone to perform a task with invisible tools or utensils; the person instructed may be real or imaginary.

Imaginary partners: The player must first establish his partner's size and form by making "eye" contact with him, taking his arm while walking, and by helping him to a chair, or by performing other simple tasks with him. Once the partner is "created," the player is assigned a teaching task such as:

Teach your partner to tie his shoelaces without making any reference to your own shoelaces.

Teach your partner to bathe or diaper a baby.

Teach your partner to ride a bike.

Variations:

Establish the imaginary partner as a baby, and teach him to eat with a spoon.

Become a driving instructor giving lessons to a young person just eligible for a driving license, or to an old person who has been driving illegally for years without one.

Establish a dog as the imaginary partner and teach it a complicated trick, or groom it and parade it at a dog show.

Real partners: One player teaches the other to play a newly invented complicated musical instrument, or to operate a complex machine.

Variations:

One partner closes his eyes and assumes the role of one blind since birth. He must be instructed to operate a simple machine — for example, a potato peeler.

One partner "becomes" deaf and must be taught meaningful words.

One partner is from a foreign country and does not understand the language. He must be taught how to operate a complicated machine. Or he must be taught all the niceties of scoring in tennis or football.

Chapter Two

SOUND PATTERNS:
RHYTHM & DRAMA

This group of lessons requires preparation by the student, and also involves "audience".

It is advisable to precede these with a discussion of rhythm and its relationship to human activities. In particular, the students should understand how rhythm in everyday activities increases efficiency, how this in turn has led to such art forms as work songs and dance, and how rhythm has become an essential element for communication in art.

Workshop 10: Sound Plots

Phase 1:

Ask one student to begin beating time regularly, like a metronome, on the floor or on a desk. While he continues this beat, ask another student to intersperse a beat between the beats of the first student. While these continue, invite others, one at a time, to add beats to the rhythm. The combination of these individual contributions should form a unique pattern which will serve as an introduction to the activities which follow.

Phase 2:

Ask the students to form groups of four or five members and prepare a sound pattern by beating on the floor or on desks. The pattern must be regular and continuous as if the beat could be repeated endlessly. Allow about five minutes preparation time and then ask each group to demonstrate their sound pattern to the class. The degree of success will vary, but the better groups will inspire the others. Students with previous musical training usually have no difficulty here for this is only a very primitive percussion band.

Phase 3:

Ask one group (preferably not the best one) to perform again, this time following your hand coaching. Agree on hand signals which will indicate start, louder, softer, faster, slower, and stop. Lead them through the pattern of a good suspense drama, becoming louder and faster up to a sub-climax, hushed before building to another one, finally leading them to a noisy climax, and then abrupt silence.

Discussion: What well-known television drama follows that kind of plot? What other plot diagrams can you remember from television and movies? How do situation comedy plot diagrams differ from those of detective thrillers?

Now each group prepares a plot, using the rhythm they have established, but having in mind a definite story line. Allow ten or fifteen minutes preparation time, and then ask the groups to perform their plot patterns. Ask the rest of the students for their opinions on the type of play they have just experienced. Some of the plots will be recognizable as specific television series; a rare one will even plot an original drama.

Phase 4:

This is the phase where the fun — and the real noise —begins. Ask the students to select objects around the room from which they can derive varieties of sound. Before they begin, make sure you outlaw any classroom equipment which might sustain permanent damage. If the selection is poor, you may wish to import a few jam cans and orange crates to act as drums. Assign the same task as in Phase 3 but give less preparation time.

This time the plots will be even more explicit because these new sound-makers will often provide sound effects rather than just a sound pattern.

Variation:

Provide the students with noisemakers, primary band percussion instruments, and penny whistles. These add more variety than found instruments and prevent damage to the classroom wastebasket, but less ingenuity is required on the part of the students.

Phase 5:

This time, the students may add vocal sounds to the other sounds they have created, but all recognizable words are disallowed. The result of this activity is a strange primitive music that is exciting to both players and audience. The discussions which follow are the most exciting of any in this series.

The questions which teachers generally ask me are: "What about the racket?" and "How do the kids hear their own group's sounds?" Well, the groups are usually concentrating so intently that few seem aware of the other noise around them. And if I as a teacher concentrate in the same way I don't hear the "racket". But what about the surrounding classrooms? After a year of this kind of teaching, you'll probably be assigned a room next to the machine shop as I was, so don't worry.

Workshop 11: Sound Patterns and Combat

Phase 1:

Divide the class into groups of five members; within each, make a division of three and two. The three are to be the beaters or directors, and the two are to be the players. Instruct the directors to prepare a sound pattern with a number of sub-climaxes and a final definite climax. Instruct the players that they may only move as the beat dictates and may only strike at each other when an emphatic beat occurs. Remind them of the rule of no contact (refer to Part One, Combat). Allow combatants their choice of mimed weapons as this gives more variety of movement. Or allow only one weapon between the combatants so that they must fight for possession of it.

Ten to fifteen minutes preparation time is usually sufficient, but circulate among the groups to coach, and warn players when they are forcing the beat instead of allowing themselves to be directed. Each fight scene should have shape — a beginning, middle and climax — just as if it were a complete drama.

Performance: the results of this activity, even with very young children, resemble a sort of underwater ballet. I don't point this out to most students, because some still find dance an embarrassment.

Variation 1:

Use the same technique, but the players' assignment is that one shall be a wild animal and the other shall be an animal trainer. Again the directors control the action, and the action must have a definite plot.

Variation 2:

The same technique, but the actors are bull and bullfighter, or butterfly and butterfly collector, or dog and cat, or a similar conflict situation.

Variation 3:

Groups are limited to four members, one director or controller for each actor. One director uses a vocal sound effect to control his player, while the other uses a beaten sound pattern. This method gives a distinctive and separate sound rhythm for each player and produces a contrast effect instead of the rhythmic dance effect of the original lesson. It is rather like operating puppets, the sound patterns being the manipulated strings.

Workshop 12: Ceremonies

The responses to the following assignments have a tendency to become stereotyped. A preliminary discussion should therefore be used to widen the viewpoint of the students.

Phase 1:

Discussion material: Man sometimes channels his emotions into rituals or ceremonies in order to conceal or control them, or make them acceptable to society. (You may wish to use the funeral ceremony as a point of departure.) Certain forms of behavior are then acceptable because they have become traditional. The students will be able, with a little prompting, to name many ceremonies with which they are familiar and in some cases be able to understand why man invented them. An example you may wish to explore in detail is the modern election ceremony with its speeches, bands and banners, cheerleaders, rallies and whistlestop tours, baby-kissing and handshaking.

Next discuss the ceremonies that primitive man may have evolve. Tribal sacrifice will usually be the first mentioned, but students should be made aware that rituals included more than just throwing your enemies into live volcanoes!

Discussion questions: How do you think worship began? Why did the early Egyptians and other early peoples worship the sun and the moon? What other things did early man worship? Why? In what ways could the very earliest prehistoric man, without material wealth, show his appreciation to the unknown being that made the sun appear each day?

Now discuss the particular ceremonies of a hypothetical tribe, which in prehistoric times might have lived on the flesh of wild animals in the jungles of Central America. Contrast these supposed ceremonies with those of a hypothetical tribe in prehistoric Siberia. Discuss the needs and conditions which would create the social patterns and eventually the rituals of these people.

Phase 2:

Divide the class into groups of six or seven members, and instruct each group to form a primitive tribe. Give them sufficient time to decide its locale, climate, economic basis, social structure, and defense system. Side coaching will help here, for the groups will tend to spend too much time on the power politics of selecting a chief, and on the tribal diet, there being an immense macabre appeal in horrid foodstuffs!

This assignment has produced some extremely interesting groups for me, among them raft-dwelling peoples, tree dwellers, and numerous variations on arctic cultures.

Phase 3:

Ask each tribe to prepare a ceremony reflecting its life style, returning once more to the use of the sound pattern. All members of the tribe are to consider themselves both directors and players, so that a sound pattern is contributed by all members and can therefore become very complex. Remind the tribes that a ceremony is channeled emotion, and that the rhythm and pattern of the sound and movement are the means by which the emotion is shaped and directed. But remind them also that the rhythm pattern is used to heighten the emotion and the theatrical impact of the ritual.

A minimum of fifteen minutes of preparation time will

be required, but groups that become really involved in the project will take much more time, perhaps more than one class session. Almost invariably the first attempt will produce grimly tragic or macabre rituals, most of them involving sacrifice. One compensation is that a large percentage of them will be compellingly beautiful in form, and the players as well as the audience will have a most powerful experience. If you'd rather complete this activity on a more optimistic note, suggest that the tribe prepare a second ceremony involving a joyous occasion, such as a successful harvest.

Phase 4:

If any of your groups is somewhat sophisticated you might suggest it try a double ceremony, such as the ushering out of winter and the welcoming of spring, or the end of the reign of an old chief and the beginning of a new chief's reign.

Phase 5:

Ask your groups to become modern "tribes", and set a modern ceremony to a sound pattern. An example that most will have experienced or at least heard about is the modern wedding employing a popular band, or one that has been staged in an unusual setting, or with unusual music or other "stage" effects.

One final note: The activities in this chapter, and especially those in the final workshop, tie in naturally with a social studies unit on primitive people, or on religion.

Chapter Three

GROUP POETRY PRODUCTION

These activities follow easily and naturally after Sound Patterns.

Workshop 13: Fabricating Vocabulary

Groups of three persons each are about the maximum size practicable for this type of activity. Pencils and paper should be available when needed.

The spirit here should definitely be tongue-in-cheek, and this usually encourages even the most inhibited to respond.

Phase 1:

Ask each group to choose a single vowel sound and two consonants, and to arrange these to form a nonsense word.

Example: dep

Ask them to form two more nonsense words which rhyme with the first one.

Example: ep   quep

They are now equipped with three single-syllable words which have rhyme and assonance, and from which they can then compose a four-line nonsense poem. The object is to find a rhythm that is constant in each line of the "poem" by combining the words in different sequences but maintaining the same number of syllables in each line.

Example: Dep ep ep ep

> *Quep dep ep dep*
> *Ep quep dep ep*
> *Quep quep quep quep*

Now ask the group to punctuate the poem to indicate its intonation and to rehearse it in choral speech form, giving it supposed meaning by the use of pauses (at periods and commas), changes in intonation (for question marks, etc.), and changes in voice quality to show mood.

> *Example:*   *Dep ep-ep-ep*
> *Quep dep-ep dep?*   *(sadly)*
> *Ep quep dep-dep,*
> *"Quep-quep! Quep-quep!"*   *(triumphantly)*

Each group should perform its finished project for the class.

Phase 2:

Now invite the groups to add a second sequence of three rhyming nonsense words to their vocabularies, and use the English articles, conjunctions, and a limited number of prepositions. The first set of fabricated words is now to be considered nouns, and the second set verbs.

> *Example: The complete vocabulary of the group would now consist of:*
>
> | | |
> |---|---|
> | *Nouns:* | *dep ep quep* |
> | *Verbs:* | *zar brar gwar* |
> | *Articles:* | *a the* |
> | *Conjunctions:* | *and but or* |
> | *Prepositions:* | *to from at off in on over around down up* |

A second, more complicated poem can now be prepared. Again, attention should be focused on the rhythm and the voice qualities used when performing the piece.

> *Example:*   *Over a quep, around a quep (whispered)*
> *The ep gwars on the dep,*
> *But the quep zars off in a dep, (spoken)*
> *And the ep brars up quep! (shouted)*

Phase 3:

To underline the rhythm, and further express the "meaning", ask the groups to invent synchronized actions to enhance the presentation of their poems. The actions will, of course, depend upon the meaning that the poets intend for their masterpieces. The effect is finally that of a chorus in mime and rhyme, moving in unison to a carefully enunciated gem of poetry in some unfamiliar language. It sounds like pure nonsense, but it does in fact illustrate vividly that communication need not rely on words alone.

Phase 4:

Invite the groups to fabricate alliterative poems. All the nouns and verbs in each line must begin with the same sound, with multisyllabic words now being allowed. The object is for the selected sounds to suggest the nature of the activities described in the poem.

> *Example:* Fio frippies furbled on the frinsorp,
> Frasset and frasset and frasset,
> And off on a finkledegompet,
> Fooble, fim-fam Fooble, fabnasset!

The alliterative sounds begin to be associated with meaning, and finally when the poems are performed with actions, sound and movement together explain the meaning.

Workshop 14: Poetry Based on Image

The poems in the first workshop will probably have a simple beat of stressed and unstressed syllables. Now you can invite the students to set up complex sound patterns as in Part Two and then to compose a poem to fit the beat (that is, the "music" first and then the words). This poem should consist of meaningful language whenever possible but may include fabricated words whenever the poets are stuck for a suitable rhyme or for onomatopocia. Again the composers should perform it either in synchronized action or in illustrative mime.

Variation 1:

Fine imagery is at the heart of poetry but student poets often hope to create pictures in the mind by tacking a couple of overused adjectives onto a noun. Invite the class to invent descriptions of chosen objects using no more than three words, none of which can be the name of the object. For example, "a small boy with a cold" became for one student "a runny-nosed sleeve-wiper". Others that have evoked interesting responses are:

> *a seagull at a garbage dump*
> *a construction worker on a high bridge*
> *Monday morning at nine o'clock*
> *a skydiver*

Students can put their responses to these on the blackboard to provide a pool of imagination for the work to follow. Now divide into groups of three or four students, each group choosing the image that they most enjoy from the board as the basis for a group poem. They must analyze the beat or sound pattern found in the image, and then construct a poem using that beat and the chosen image. Encourage them to include other images from the board or to compose descriptions that complement the original image chosen. Once again the poem is to be performed with suitable actions for the class.

Variation 2:

Invite each group to invent advertising jingles for mythical products. They may fabricate words to describe the magic ingredients and their supernatural attributes. The jingles may be performed in the manner of a fried chicken commercial.

Variation 3:

Prepare nursery rhymes as if they were cheers to spur on the school football team.

Workshop 15: Poetic Drama

This is primarily for more confident students as it involves a certain amount of individual performance. The groups may be slightly larger for this, with as many as four or five members.

Phase 1:

The assignment is to prepare rhyming dialog and perform it as a brief play. The easiest introduction to this is through assigning a specific plot to be performed in a standard comic style. The ideal plot: the kidnap and subsequent rescue of a bee-*oo*-tiful maiden. The perfect style for the purpose: meller-drammer. Both plot and style allow for wild exaggeration and may be attacked with gusto. Encourage the students to include terrible puns and outrageous rhymes in their scripts. Response to this assignment has always been tremendously enthusiastic.

Phase 2:

The same assignment, but challenge the students to invent an original plot to be presented in serious style. This is much more difficult but with more confident groups the results can be very successful.

Phase 3:

Invite the groups to invent a plot in which the characters always work in pairs. Thus two bank robbers are foiled by two clever bank clerks. In this assignment, whenever possible the two robbers will speak together and the two clerks will speak in unison, with variations using alternating dialog where one finishes the other's thoughts.

> *Example:*   *JOE & HARRY (in handcuffs):*
>
>   *We gave a solemn promise to mother that we'd never ever break da law,*
>
> *JOE:*   *But how could I turn down me brother when he needed some cash to withdraw?*
>
> *HARRY:*   *And I'm sure it would please us both, mother,*
>
> *JOE:*   *If you sent us a cake . . .*
>
> *HARRY:*   *. . . with a saw!*

I have seen groups so thoroughly involved in this assignment that they end up with a full-scale production.

Chapter Four

GROUP ACTIVITIES

These activities are inspired by various art forms, music, and patterns of light, sometimes separately, sometimes in combination. Most of these workshops divide the class at some point into groups, and finally require some form of performance and audience reaction or participation. The depth of the discussions which follow various phases of these activities will depend upon the maturity and sophistication of the groups.

Workshop 16: Drama Activity
Inspired by Music and Pictures

Prepare six or eight collages. They should be large enough to be easily visible to the entire class (perhaps 30 by 40 inches). Use a strong cement to fasten the selected articles onto cardboard or thin plywood. Nothing ruins this activity more efficiently than a deteriorating inspiration so be sure they are on there securely. If the collages are well made, they can be used again and again, or can become a permanent part of the room decor.

Each collage should have a basic unity within it so that it will not suggest too many ambiguous or confused connotations to the class. Collages may be prepared entirely of textiles. Unity may be gained by types of texture; one collage may include sandpaper, burlap, rope, raffia, terry-toweling, rough plaster, and steel wool; another may include fur, absorbent cotton, knitted wool, flannelette, foam rubber, and feathers. Unity may also be gained by using shades of a single color, or a limited group of colors. Or the materials used may all be cut in similar shapes, very angular, curved or in strips.

Collages may also be prepared from natural objects such as leaves, seeds, shells and wood. But again a degree of unity must be maintained in the selection of the objects, relating those of a specific environment, or size, or quality.

Variation:

If circumstances permit, groups of students may prepare the collages to begin this workshop, but they must be directed to keep a theme in mind as they work. In subsequent phases of the activity, each group can concentrate on its own collage.

Phase 1:

Display the collages along one wall of the classroom, or at least close enough to one another so that your students can compare them readily. Select three or four pieces of contrasting music (see Appendix). Ask your students to examine the collages as a piece of music is played and to select a collage that "goes with" or "works best with" the music. Play each of the pieces, leaving a brief time for thinking between them.

Discussion: Which collage did you choose for Music No. 1? Why did you choose it? How did it fit the music? What words describe the feeling in the music and in its collage? Can you make movements with your hands which describe or express this feeling? What emotions are involved? What experiences were you reminded of? What kinds of drama were suggested?

It's obvious that there will be great variations in reactions, although in some instances an almost unanimous verdict may result. Some students may appreciate the subtle differences in music and be eager to point out the incongruities between the music and certain details in the collage they have chosen to go with it. Others will intuitively connect the "shape" of the music and the shapes of the forms in the collage. Still others may experience a complete play scenario during the music.

Phase 2:

Select a new piece of music, preferably one markedly different from those used in Phase 1. Divide the class into groups of three or four students. Instruct the groups to listen to the music to be played while studying the collages, and then to discuss quietly within their group a locale or setting suggested to them by the collage and the music combined. Occasionally a group will not be able to agree on a single collage, but group work requires compromise and cooperation so allow them to resolve their own dilemma as far as possible.

Now instruct the groups that they are to become characters within their chosen setting and that something will "happen" to them as the music dictates. Play the selection again while the students decide their roles and the outline of their plot. Specify whether the play is to be mimed or whether dialog is to be allowed.

Replays of the music will be necessary so that the players can plot their action more precisely to the demands of the music. This is especially necessary if the work is to be mimed. Finally, the productions should be ready for sharing with the class. Many will have chosen the same collage; some will even have chosen the identical locale; even the characters may be the same. But every play will be unique in some way because the players are unique.

Discussion: Audience: which collage do you think this play was based on? Players: which collage did you actually choose? Why? What elements suggested these characters? What elements suggested the mood? What elements were most at odds with the drama performed?

Variation 1:

For a different visual stimulus, use reproductions of portraits by famous artists, or large photographs of persons clipped from slick magazines, especially the photos used in advertisements. Alter the instructions by asking the students to match the characters with the music first, then decide mood, locale and plot. Groups might best be limited to two persons each, one representing the character portrayed and the other a person to whom he relates. Or each group can be given a chart showing more than one character.

Variation 2:

Use reproductions of famous art works as visual stimuli. One of the best sources of these is the Reinhold Visuals* which

Reference: Reinhold Visuals (Aids for Art Teaching)
    Reinhold Book Corporation, New York, London.

may already be in some school libraries. These include photographs of ancient and modern sculpture and may be used in exactly the same way as the collages.

Variation 3:

For visual stimuli, use objects which have interesting shapes, colors, and textures. You can use grotesquely arranged foam rubber, derelict machinery, collections of balloons or other toys, hats, shoes or other wearing apparel, branches and flowers, or rocks and shells. These can be displayed individually, or arranged in still-life groups. With such stimuli, you can vary the instructions, having the articles represent either the locale or the characters involved.

Variation 4:

For auditory stimuli, use sound effects. Recordings of the engines of planes and automobiles provide material to prepare your own taped sequences like movie sound tracks. Continuous recordings of birdsong, ocean waves, or wind also provide good background sound for dramatic plots. Or the sounds may be a sequence of normally unrelated sources, producing an op-art effect. Or you can prepare a sound effects tape by recording the noises available in your own kitchen, such as those of your blender, coffee percolator, washing machine, dishwasher, and electric timer. Also available are interesting recordings of insect sounds in which many of the sounds are magnified and slowed down for closer study, and the effects are rather surrealistic.

Workshop 17: Drama Activity Involving Light Sources

For this type of work, the room must have shades which will eliminate most outdoor light. The light sources used may be flashlights, small desk lamps, or shaded bulbs on extension cords, but in any case they must be portable and must have a directed beam.

Phase 1:

The class should be divided into groups of four or five students, and each group provided with a light source. You may, however, have to limit the groups to the number of electrical outlets or light sources available. Each group will also require three pieces of theatrical gelatine — amber, red and blue. Ask them to experiment with the lights and gels examining hands, books, eyeglasses, and pencils in different colored light and at different angles of light. Ask them to watch the shadow effects and the effect of using two different gels to divide the light source.

Variation:

You may introduce this activity with one large group around a single table, to stimulate a general discussion from which all class members may benefit. However, the large size of the class may make this system ineffective.

Phase 2:

Ask students to take turns posing in the light so that others may see the effect of lighting from different angles, noting how mood changes with changes in the direction of the light and in its color.

Discussion: If you wish to suggest that a character is sad, what gel would you use? If the mood is happy, or one of revolt, or of disappointment, where might you place the light source in relation to the subject? What color will you use?

Phase 3:

Each group will require a second light source, more gels, some aluminum foil to form cones to channel the light beams, and some masking tape to fasten the gels to the cones. Warn the students to avoid fire hazard by not placing the gels too close to the heat of the light source. The assignment is to prepare a still life using their own bodies and/or any objects or furniture they find in the room, and employing their lighting equipment to enhance the project and heighten its mood. You may suggest a specific mood or emotion or theme for each group, or you may wish to let each group evolve its own as it goes along.

Phase 4:

The students may now prepare an improvisation based on the still life, at some time in the plot employing the exact pose and lighting that they have created in the still life arrangement.

Variation:

If numerous light sources are not available, fasten two or three lights to a portable coat stand and allow each group a turn with the lights. This is, of course, only a last resort as those who are waiting tend to occupy themselves in rather nonproductive activity.

Workshop 18: Drama Activity Using Music and Light

Phase 1:

Select a number of recordings or tapes of mood music, each short piece chosen to contrast with the others (see Appendix). Obtain a selection of theatrical gels, varying through the shades of reds and purples to soft amber.

Using a single light source, change the gels in front of the light as a portion of each of the musical selections is played until the class is generally satisfied with one or two shades of color appropriate for each selection. The matching of color and light will often contradict decisions made about mood in Workshop 2, because music will change the values.

Phase 2:

Divide the class into three or four groups, assigning each a light source. Allow the group to select a colored gel and one of the music selections. They are to prepare a mimed improvisation or a dance mime appropriate to the rhythm of their chosen music and the mood of their lighting. You will have to play portions of each required selection repeatedly, so that the groups can take time alternately to plan and to rehearse to their musical accompaniment.

If you have the equipment, using cassette recordings for this is ideal for the groups may play their own music as they require it. You may even find other work areas in the school for them to prepare their scenes.

Anything more than ninety minutes work on this workshop will be self-defeating; the improvisations become stale and the players bored.

Workshop 19: Lighted Table-Top Sets

This activity is only feasible if you have access to pieces of colored fabric at least a couple of yards long. Colored paper can be made to serve but is not as effective because it lacks fabric's flexibility. You will also require a collection of odd-shaped and textured articles, such as hand mirrors, spools, bottles, old jewelry, bits of fur, driftwood, shells, bones, eyeglasses, small boxes, egg cartons, tubes from wrapping paper, and balls.

Phase 1:

Examine all the objects under various colors and angles of light. Group several objects in different arrangements and play light on them from different angles. Discuss the effects gained.

Phase 2:

Examine the colored fabric under colored light, to see the changes in the shades obtained. Create "mountains" and other topographical variations in the fabric and discuss the landscapes obtained, and how direction and color of light alter the effects.

Phase 3:

Divide into groups and allow each group to select a piece of fabric, half a dozen objects, a light source, and some gelatines. Their assignment is to prepare a tabletop set or landscape which will tell a story to the viewer.

Phase 4:

Visit each set with the entire class. Have the audience discuss the impressions they get from the landscape: What story do they read there? Next ask the creators to discuss the story they had hoped to express in their landscape.

Variation:

Some groups may wish to add music to their presentation to heighten the mood, especially if the activities immediately preceding this assignment involved some really evocative music that they can now associate with this new project.

Table-top sets have an advantage over some of the other activities described here: they are fairly quiet.

Chapter Five

IMPROVISATIONS WITH LARGE GROUPS

It is desirable, at least some of the time, for the class to be involved in a common large group experience, all the members participating in a single improvised event. The following activities therefore do not specifically divide the class into performers and audience, although all members alternate in both capacities during most of the proceedings.

Be very sure of your ability to control the situation before you introduce this type of activity.

The improvisations are of two kinds — imposed situations and semi-structured happenings. The first are planned by the teacher, with chosen stimuli, primarily musical, molding the reactions of the participants. The second are those in which a general situation is described and the students in discussion decide on the specific action, their roles in it, and the details of the setting in which the action will occur. Or the characters are suggested, and the setting imposed, and the students in discussion decide the plot. After this, the events in the dramas are propelled along by the interaction of these elements.

Workshop 20: Imposed Situations

This usually involves mime only, and is motivated by music.

Phase 1:

This first example is the simplest one given. Ask your students to find an acting area and sit comfortably. Explain that written into the course of the music you are going to play (see Appendix) is a disaster, either natural or man-made, in which they will all be involved. Ask them to remain where they are when the music begins until they can imagine their roles and the setting. After that, although no speech may be used, they may interact with others if they wish or they may remain isolated. Each student is to interpret the situation in his own way. He will often misinterpret the roles he sees others playing, because he will judge their actions in the light of the setting he has imagined — but this is, after all, very similar to what happens in life; we do interpret the actions of others in accordance with our own experiences.

One selection that is most successful for this improvisation is Pink Floyd's *Saucerful of Secrets*. It begins with electronic music, swells to an overwhelming crescendo of rolling explosion, and then is subtly transformed into organ music giving it an almost religious quality in the closing portion. However, any good electronic music will be suitable for this improvisation as long as it includes some section that builds to a powerful climax. Then try to make sure that the final portion is serene to allow relief from tensions that might build up.

Phase 2:

Discussion of the events occurring in the improvisation.

Variation 1:

Use the same technique, but this time the students are informed that they are the earliest primitive men and have yet to make any discoveries about their environment. In the course of the music provided, they must find food, or shelter, or a body covering, and in doing it must cope with their surroundings. Instruct them not to anticipate or force action, for all the clues should come from the music (see Appendix). No speech may occur between the participants for, of course, man has not yet discovered speech. (This is a slightly sneaky method of getting a quiet session!)

Choosing the music is not quite as difficult as it sounds for if you are told that the music has certain qualities, you are inclined to find them in it. There are some good movie sound tracks made for jungle pictures, or you may prepare your own tape using wind sound effects, wild animals and birds calling, electrical storm effects, and tie it all together with some good electronic music.

Variation 2:

Prepare three or four selections of music which will form a story pattern that travels to several locales or through several phases. An example might be that of a lion hunt, which could begin with jungle music, continue with seagoing music, then circus music, and finally back to jungle music again to return the lion to his home.

Prepare a collection of costume accessories and hand properties suitable for the occasion. Spread them out where they can be readily appreciated by the players, while you preview the music for them. In discussion, decide on a sequence of settings. The story line will almost automatically take shape from student suggestions. Next come decisions on the characters involved and the roles to be assigned to each player. Everyone in the class must be involved in some manner.

Divide the room into the necessary action areas and arrange furniture to suggest the settings. Now play the music once more while the students work out more details of the plot, and judge the length of time that the action must take to fit the music. Allow players to select properties and costume accessories to fit their roles, and you are ready for the grand performance. In a rather informal way, students waiting their turn to become involved in the action are the audience.

The first time this type of extended activity is attempted, the burden is placed on the teacher to provide an adequate scenario and sound track. But when the activity is to be repeated, the players will be ready to select a topic, divide it into segments, and perhaps suggest appropriate music. They'll probably want to contribute properties and costume accessories too, without any prompting.

Variation 3:

Use tape recordings of a series of sound effects, preferably in groups of three or four related sounds (for example: a foghorn, ocean waves, and seagulls) followed several minutes later by two or three more groups of sounds. Let the class prepare a story which takes advantage of each group of sound effects and each silence in succession. The spaces between the sound effects allow a more leisurely pace to the plot.

Workshop 21: Semi-Structured Happenings

All of the situations described in this workshop require dialog; music may be used during the improvisation or before to set the mood but it is not mandatory.

The Old Folks Home.

The setting is described to the class as a home for the aged and infirm. The building is inadequate for its purpose, and the staff too few in number. This is the starting point for discussion. Begin by having the students consider what it is like to be very aged and/or chronically ill, and what it is like to feel unnecessary. Have them discuss what temperaments the staff members might have, what their duties would be, and what the daily routine would include. Have them describe the building and its grounds.

The students must decide what part of the room will represent the building, what part the grounds. More mature groups will be specific about doorways, individual rooms, and even pathways in the garden area.

Next, roles are chosen, and the play begins. Students are to maintain their characters, speaking only as the personality they have assumed. Individual activities and small interactions occur but inevitably these begin to escalate until finally all the players become involved in an "event". Break off the improvisation when the students generally break out of character, or the event has spent its force.

Discussion should follow, but don't let it become a fault-finding session. The success of this activity depends on the group's maturity and knowledge of the problems of the aged. The younger the group, the less serious will be the approach.

Variation 1:   Prisoner-of-War Camp or Prison

Discuss the chow line, mail call, bunkhouse or cell restrictions, guard duties, methods of escape possible, and methods of preventing escape. As in the preceding, decide the players' roles and map out the setting.

Remind the students about the rule for staged violence: "No physical contact is to be made in fight sequences." With more rambunctious groups it is sometimes sensible to impose the "slow-motion-fights only" rule also.

Variation 2: A Soup Kitchen During the Depression

Discuss the conditions under which people who have been long out of work must live, and their reaction to charity. Discuss the kinds of people who might work in the soup kitchen and their reactions to the unemployed who come there.

Variation 3: The New Settlement

A group of settlers around the year 1800 head west and select a site for a farming community. Discuss the order of priority for building homes, barns, a meeting house and a stockade, land clearing, planting, weaving, soap-making, etc. Discuss the types of persons involved in the venture, their responsibilities, and the dangers which surround them.

Variation 4: The Fortress

This is a slight variation on the preceding. A group of medieval traders find themselves shipwrecked on an unfamiliar treeless land. They must establish a stone fortress or castle for defense for there is no lumber to build a ship with which to sail home, and they must be prepared to defend themselves against marauding barbarians who infest the surrounding country. Winter is coming and the traders must strive for survival. Discuss group organization, their tools, the type of structure they might build, and their provisions for the coming winter.

Variation 5: The Sailing Ship

The setting is a trading ship during the days of pirates, carrying molasses and rum from Jamaica to New England. Discuss shipboard duties, crew organization, and the dangers of the journey such as shifting cargo, storms, mutiny, epidemics, and, of course, pirates.

Variation 6: Train Robbery

A group of pioneer men driven to desperate measures by the near starvation of their families, rob a train traveling from a gold mine.

Variation 7:

The trial of the men responsible for the train robbery.

Variation 8:   The Dig

Archaeologists excavating in the deserts of North Africa (or the jungles of Central America) discover an ancient city. Groups become local tribesmen, excavators, would-be thieves, government inspectors, representatives of the news media.

Variation 9:   The Tribe

Anthropologists in the jungles of the East Indian islands discover a primitive tribe which has never been in contact with civilization. It might help here to discuss the reports on the Tasaday tribe discovered in the Phillipines in 1971. However, the Tasadays' reactions to civilization are not necessarily the only possible reactions.

Variation 10:   The Bus Tour

A private club of retired people (or school teachers, or dentists' wives) is traveling towards Mexico or New York. Players will become tour guides, drivers, hotel and restaurant workers and gas station operators.

Variation 11:   The Picnic

The annual picnic in Vancouver of the expatriate Americans from Alabama. Players become picnic organizers, speech makers, newest and oldest members.

Variation 12:   After the Hijack

The arrival of the passengers at an airport after a hijacking attempt. Players become pilot and crew, hijackers, police, newsmen, crash crew, injured passengers, insurance representatives, families of the passengers.

Variation 13:   The Feud

A feud between two families. Players become heads of the families, lawyers, police. Discuss the reasons for the feud, and place the setting for the events.

Variation 14:   Trapped!

The safe rescue of people trapped in a cave. Discuss their reasons for being in the cave, why it has become sealed, the layout of the cave, and methods of rescue. Players become police, firemen, mine engineers, trapped victims, anxious families, and newsmen.

Workshop 22: Semi-Structured Happenings: Junk Character Encounters

This workshop may be repeated at intervals during the school year, substituting fresh "junk" each time. The activity never fails to inspire some very original work.

Phase 1:

Introduce a single junk item to the class, perhaps a wooden fishing float, a piece of an engine, a gourd, a broken basket, an old wine bottle, or some other junked item with definite character. This item represents a character; he (she) must receive a name from the class, and have his (her) personality described according to the qualities of the object. For the wine bottle, he would, of course, have once been full (of promise?) and life has drained him; as he is transparent, one can "see right through him". The class must also decide on a fitting occupation for him.

Another junk character is then introduced and personalized in the same way.

Phase 2:

A setting for an enounter between these two characters is now decided upon, two volunteer players take on the roles described, and the play begins. The object is to make a simple encounter into a complete play with a distinct form, relying on the characteristics of the two junk people to carry the action.

Phase 3:

Students pair off, each one choosing a junk article from those available (the more the better). They enact an encounter and the audience must watch closely to decide the characteristics being portrayed. Later discussion centers on interpretation of the junk articles' qualities as portrayed in the scene.

Variation 1:

Use hats instead of junk. The hat is now worn by the

character and its qualities define the characteristics which must guide the player's actions and reactions in the encounter. The player must be aware that the hat is not only his costume but it also embodies the very character that he must portray.

Variation 2:

Use hand properties instead of junk. These may include clocks, telephones, canes, telescopes, tools and books. The article, in addition to defining the character, must be used in the plot of the encounter. The telephone-person, for example, uses the telephone in the scene, but he also has its qualities: smooth, automated, sensitive to sound.

Variation 3:

Define the encounter setting first. Be specific. "A stalled elevator between the 17th and 18th floors of an office tower at 6 p.m. on a Friday during an elevator repairmen's strike" or "the only two to show up for the high school reunion picnic on a rainy day at the Happy Holiday Resort". Now determine the characters using any of the above methods.

Phase 4:

By now the players should be familiar enough with the techniques to be ready for Rotating Encounters. This uses any of the above methods for starters, but the original characters in the scene may be joined by other players at random. After the encounter begins, it may continue as long as the players can invent new action. Entry into the action by new players simply involves selecting a character hat (or junk item, or property), an acceptable means of involvement for the character, and a suitable time of entry. The number of players on "stage" at any one time may be limited to four or five, by requiring that player No. 1 find an exit for his character when player No. 6 makes an entry. Unmotivated entries or those that ruin a good plot sequence are usually subtly denounced by audience reaction. Students who have previously developed a sensitive reaction to one another almost instinctively know when to join the play.

Workshop 23: Semi-Structured Happenings: Take-Off!

Take-off is a rather complicated improvised game for

students who have worked together for some time and who have a fairly wide command of language. The basic rules for the game are given below; you can add twists to it as your students become adept.

Phase 1:

Choose a setting and a conflict situation for an improvisation. Ask for two volunteer players who will begin the scene. Pair off the remaining class members, and appoint a referee. The students sit in a large circle, each beside his partner.

Phase 2:

The volunteer pair begins an improvisation in the center of the circle. At any interesting point in the dialog, the referee stops the action (use a whistle if you like!). The "audience" must consider the last line of dialog spoken, and silently choose any word and/or portion of a word from it on which to base a new improvisation. Slight distortions of the word chosen are allowed or even encouraged; the emphasis is on the sounds heard rather than on the words themselves.

The hard part comes next: A new pair of players must use the word or sound with a different meaning than that in which they heard it used, they must use it within the first speech of the improvisation, and they must begin the improvisation *without* the advantage of consultation with one another. The first new pair of players to decide (silently!) on a new improvisation moves into the center of the circle and begins its scene.

> *Example: First pair's improvisation*
>
> *Setting:* a park
> *Characters: No. 1 — a man with a cigarette and no match*
> *No. 2 — a man with a match*
>
> *Player No. 1:* Hey, mister, you got a light?
> *Player No. 2:* Who, me?
> *Player No. 1:* Yeh, you! You got a light?
> *Player No. 2:* You want a light from me?
> *Player No. 1:* Yeh, I want a light for this here cigarette.
> *Player No. 2:* Well, even if I had a light, I wouldn't

                                    give it to you!
         Player No. 1:   *Why not? Hey, whatsamatter with you,*
                            anyhow?

STOP ACTION.

   The new improvisation must make use of any word and/or
portion of word heard in the last line — "Why not? Hey, whatsamatter with you anyhow" — but must use the word with a
different meaning.

   Thus, a new player could begin a scene with:

   "Look here you, you've drunk the last of the wine!" (Why
not)
   or: *"We'll have to get this hay in before it rains!" (Hey)*
   or: *"Did you shake out that mat, Mary?" (whatsamatter)*
   or: *"Did you say your name was Sam?" (whatsamatter)*

   Gradually the reactions will come faster and faster, the
competition keener, and the double meanings used wittier.
Some of the puns will elicit groans from the audience!

   Just one caution here: the players must be reminded constantly that dialog alone does not constitute a play; they *must*
include action.

Part II

DRAMATIC SKETCHES

AUTHOR'S NOTE

Many of the sketches in this book are the result of the frustrations of trying to find short, complete-in-themselves acting scripts for a group of exceptional young actors with whom I worked. In preparing them, I kept in mind production feasibility and small cast size suitable for these actors. But it soon became apparent that the sketches are also appropriate for any small theatrical group and for informal drama workshop presentations.

*It is not uncommon for an acting class in a public school to number 25 or 30 members, all of them eager to participate. With such a class I find that the learning situation is richer if several groups are working on a single play at the same time. It's quite possible, for example, to have three casts of **Sophie**, two of **Fortunes**, and four of **Tea Party** operating simultaneously. The actors will have the advantage not only of learning from each others' mistakes, but also of experiencing a few more of the infinite interpretations of a single role. In a cooperative classroom environment where criticism is positive, this type of assignment will not promote undue competition. Rather, it tends to foster real concern for and discussion of more creative approaches to acting and higher standards of work.*

In using the production notes at the beginning of each play, you will find that the suggestions for preparation involve the entire class. Then, if you open each new class session with a different type of preparation, all members will benefit, not just those involved in a particular sketch. All of the preparations, although keyed to specific plays, are valuable for any acting assignment.

Each sketch requires minimum stage settings and properties, uncomplicated costumes, and, with a couple of exceptions, very basic lighting and sound effects. At the beginning of each play, I have suggested staging that will be workable and inexpensive, but there are, of course, many alternatives for elaboration which will suggest themselves to the director.

*Both **Tea Party** and **Down on Your Knees** seem to demand some period stage furnishings. But a few pieces, a small table and a sofa perhaps, will usually suffice for the setting. **Bridgework** requires a horn but these can be bought in joke and party shops. The lighting in **Walking Back** could prove troublesome if facilities are too limited, but simply performing in reduced light, or positioning the light source so that the* woman's place of appearance and disappearance is in shadow should establish the mood. Properties in **Mr. Excelsior** and **Down on Your Knees** may appear difficult because carpentry tools and silver ornaments are only reluctantly loaned. However, in every basement there is at least one discarded or unrepairable tool and in every attic at least one horrendous wedding present. Appeals for friends' attic and basement treasures usually produce fine results. The fog in **Perfect Perley** may be supplied by a pan of dry ice and a fan.

Eleven of the sketches require only two actors. **Tea Party** has three but one is only a walk-on, **Fortunes'** third actor is silent, and only in **Down on Your Knees** do three actors participate fully. My intention was that the actors should concentrate on one-to-one relationships in this group of plays, for even these are extremely complex. Therefore, even in the three-actor sketches the relationship is actually two-way. In **Down on Your Knees,** Ab is a surrogate father for Martha, and in **Fortunes,** the conflict is between the mother and the old man, although he never speaks. In **Tea Party,** although Alma and Hester bicker, they are really in conflict with the uncaring world outside represented by the boy.

All these sketches are a comment on relationships, those strings that bind person to person and thereby change and warp or enhance personalities. Some deal with mere encounters as in **Mr. Excelsior** or **The Victim,** and some with the prolonged agony of a fraying family tie as in **Trick Doors** or **Down on Your Knees.** But each one is a momentary contact with the relationship so formed and the reaction of the participants in the relationship. It is intended then, that the actors may investigate the corners of the conflicts which result, analyzing the characteristics which force confrontations, and that the audience members may share in turn in the investigation.

Finally, a note on my biases. I had planned to help increase the number of short roles available for female actors, but find that I have provided only thirteen roles for women and seventeen for men. However, there is a compensation. Only six of the female characters are losers, while there are ten male losers. (Make that eleven if you count Philip in **Winnifred and Grace**.) A third bias I admit to is one for unsettled endings. The blissful finality of happily-ever-after will not be found in these sketches, not because I am naturally pessimistic, but because I prefer to feel that the ends are far beyond these pages.

Holed-Up

Cast:

One man   *One woman*

Production Notes

In this sketch, Ralph is the epitome of undeveloped manhood, a naive youth determined to succeed in the glamorous and exciting newspaper world. He has probably held this job for a whole week, but stands little chance of holding it for a second one if all his interviews follow the course of this one.

Mrs. Gutkin, his adversary, for that she certainly is, does not care for fame. She does her job in her own fashion, and she can do without Ralph Wiggins and The Daily Guff. She is equally unimpressed by the authority of Mr. Watkins, as shown in the ashtray she has carefully stowed under the desk for her nightly cigar. Ralph's interruption of this illicit ritual is, for a few minutes, most annoying. However, she is calm and stoical in the knowledge that all things come to those who wait. And they do. Wiggins places himself in the most appropriate spot for his own elimination and she eliminates him.

It would be interesting to see her facial expressions but the audience is confined to a view of her hindquarters. Since she remains immobile for most of the sketch, the actor playing the role must make the most of her intriguing costume (perhaps a pair of silk bloomers would add a certain dazzlement), and the fact that the audience is constantly anticipating her emergence.

With this competition, what are the chances for the actor playing Wiggins? His nervous energy and silly one-sided interviewing are not sufficient. But don't sidestep the problem by giving him buck-teeth, prominent warts, and/or glasses. He shouldn't need character props if he remembers always that he *must* get a story or he'll be fired. Wiggins didn't see the hold-up but he knows what must have occurred partly from the teller's story, and partly from his own imagination. It is on this story that the actor must concentrate. He must see the events in his mind's eye and recreate them as he tells the story to Mrs. Gutkin. After all, his real intention in interviewing her is simply to confirm the story he intends to write, whether it is accurate or not. His whole attention must be on the story he is telling and enacting; he must visualize the events in order to involve the audience in it. Unless his attention is completely on those events, audience eyes will stray to that immobile posterior.

Preparation: Have the actors practice telling a series of actually experienced events to a series of listeners. Each time the events are described, the actor must add more gestures and actions. Criticism should be given by the listener every time he cannot clearly visualize the events being described.

Use the technique described in *Junk Encounters* (Workshop 22) to develop characters for Ralph and Mrs. Gutkin. Experiment with different objects as the basis for the characters in improvised scenes together and with other characters they might meet — for example, Ralph with Ruth, Mrs. Gutkin with Mr. Watkins, Ralph with his editor, Mrs. Gutkin with the robbers.

Holed-Up

Time: Late evening.

Scene: The interior of a bank at night as seen from the employees' side of the counter. The counter runs diagonally from DL to UR. On the Downstage side of the counter is a sign: "EMPLOYEES: POSITIVELY NO SMOKING. Signed Mr. Watkins". A door UL beyond the counter is the entrance to the bank from the street. DR is the door to the bank vault. The Downstage area is furnished with desks, chairs, office machines, typewriters, etc. Center stage is a secretary's desk facing Upstage. The audience can therefore see that in the leg space under the desk is crouched a person, the hindquarters of which are covered in a print dress, the feet encased in sneakers and woolen socks. This is MRS. GUTKIN and later when more of her emerges, she will be seen to be also wearing a much abused cardigan. She is in her later middle life (to put it delicately). At rise there is considerable animation to the portion of her anatomy seen by the audience. Leaning against the desk which harbors her is a mop, beside it a pail.

Enter UL, RALPH WIGGINS, conservative sports jacket, conservative tie, conservative haircut. He uses a key to enter and locks the door again after himself.

MRS. GUTKIN's posterior ceases movement as he makes his entrance: she is listening. She begins a slight backing out movement, changes her mind and burrows back into her hole.

RALPH: *(Softly, as he approaches the counter)* **Mrs. Gutkin?** *(Neither movement nor sound from under the desk.)* **Mrs. Gutkin? I know you're in here. One of the tellers, the blond with the thin legs, you know the one? Is her name Ruth maybe? Well, she loaned me her key to get in here. Of course, you're going to tell me that that is very irregular and you're right, Mrs. Gutkin, you're very right, but I explained why I wanted to see you, Mrs. Gutkin,**

1   **and she agreed with me that it was very necessary that**
2   **I get in here tonight.** *(No response.)* **Mrs. Gutkin?** *(Pause)*
3   **Mrs. Gutkin, I'm Ralph Wiggins of** *The Daily Guff*
4   **and . . .** *(Pause)* **Mrs. Gutkin, I wish you'd . . .** *(Stops, goes*
5   *around DL end of counter, doesn't find her behind the counter.*
6   *Puzzled, he goes to left of desk, and discovers her posterior.)* **Ah,**
7   **there you are, Mrs. Gutkin!** *(Extending his hand)* **I'm Ralph**
8   **Wiggins of** *The Daily Guff* **and I'd . . .** *(The posterior does not*
9   *acknowledge him. He looks at his hand foolishly, withdraws it*
10   *and pockets it.)* **. . . of** *The Daily Guff* **and I'd like to**
11   **interview you about the robbery this evening. Now I**
12   **know you haven't told your story to anyone, Mrs. Gutkin,**
13   **and I'm quite sure I could make it worth your while to**
14   **give an exclusive to** *The Daily Guff.* *(Pause)* **Financially,**
15   **that is. Financially worth your while.** *(No reply.)* **Mrs.**
16   **Gutkin?** *(He goes to tap her on the posterior, but thinks better*
17   *of it.)* **Mrs. Gutkin, I wish you'd come out and talk to me.**
18   *(Gets a chair and seats himself DL of desk opening.)* **Or anyhow**
19   **just talk to me. You don't even have to come out, Mrs.**
20   **Gutkin, just answer a few questions from in there.** *(Gets*
21   *out a notebook and pen.)* **As a matter of fact, you don't even**
22   **have to say anything; I'll just ask the questions and you**
23   **just nod your head yes or no . . .** *(Pause. He rethinks that*
24   *one.)* **Or something . . . Mrs. Gutkin, I know you were very**
25   **frightened by the robbery. That teller with the thin**
26   **legs . . . Ruth is her name? . . . she told me that you'd been**
27   **just terrified and afterwards she couldn't find you**
28   **anywhere. I know you must be still very frightened but**
29   **maybe if you'd just talk to me about it, you'd feel better.**
30   **Sort of unburden yourself, you know.** *(Pause)* **Mrs.**
31   **Gutkin?** *(Pause. He goes around desk, tries to see under it from*
32   *the Upstage side.)* **Mrs. Gutkin?** *(Moving to stage L)* **Of course,**
33   **I already know some of the story. Ruth . . . is that her**
34   **name? . . . the blond teller, she told me how the robbers**
35   **entered as she was leaving for the day.** *(He runs back to*

door UL.) **Just pushed her aside, she said, slammed her into the wall!** *(He demonstrates with bad-guy bravado.)* **Then one of them turned, brutally snatched her keys and ... LOCKED the door again!** *(Demonstrates)* **Then** *(Warming dramatically to his subject)* **"Awright, everybody freeze!" one of them said ... the fat one I believe she said. Or maybe she said it was the sickly one with the shotgun? Well, anyhow, he said "everybody freeze!" and everybody froze! And then one of them, the fat one, I think, vaulted over the counter.** *(He attempts to demonstrate this but fails.)* **Maybe it was the sickly one with the shotgun? But then his gun would have got in his way! Anyway the fat athletic one got over the counter.** *(He runs around the counter to stand in the spot where the robber would have presumably landed.)* **He pulled out a paper bag from his pocket. "Fill this!" he snarled at the bank manager. That was Mr. Watkins, of course. "Fill this, Watkins, or the dames die!"** *(Knocks the chair DL across the stage bad-guy fashion. He becomes MR. WATKINS.)* **"Please don't shoot, I'll get the money you want but it's all in the vault!"** *(Indicates vault.)* **Roughly seizing the old man, they tied him and all the tellers including the blond one ... Ruth? ... to chairs. And then they put tape over their mouths.** *(Rapidly demonstrates.)* **Now the coast was clear. They marched to the vault laughing confidently.** *(Laughs confidently on his way to the vault. He puts his hand on the door and it swings open.)* **Oh, it's still open!** *(Alarmed, then pleased that he can continue his story, he enters the vault, leaving the door open. He continues from within the vault.)* **Wildly they scooped up the loot, stuffing it into their sack, oblivious to their danger.** *(Sticks head out of the vault, and grins in the direction of MRS. GUTKIN.)* **That's where you came in, Mrs. Gutkin, right?** *(He returns to the vault, as the posterior stirs; MRS. GUTKIN backs out of her hideout and rises, a cigar clamped in her teeth.)* **You just let yourself into the bank as usual to do your**

1   **nightly cleaning . . . My goodness, haven't cleaned in here**
2   **for awhile, have you? . . . Just look at that dust, will you!**
3   *(MRS. GUTKIN marches to the vault door.)* **Well, anyhow,**
4   **you just marched in, walked right past everybody sitting**
5   **there all tied up. Just marched over and slammed that**
6   **vault door!** *(She slams the door, turns the dial on the face.)*
7   **Mrs. Gutkin? Oh, you've joined in! Right! That's exactly**
8   **right! That's exactly what you did, Mrs. Gutkin! You**
9   **slammed the door and . . . turned . . . the . . . Mrs. Gutkin?**
10   **Mrs. Gutkin, I'd like to come out now . . .** *(MRS. GUTKIN*
11   *goes back under the desk; from the secret ledge under the desk*
12   *brings out an ashtray of comfortable proportions. She backs out,*
13   *settles on the floor, leaning against the desk. She lights her cigar,*
14   *and places the ashtray on her lap.)*
15
16
17
18
19
20
21
22
23
24
25
26
27
28
29
30
31
32
33
34
35

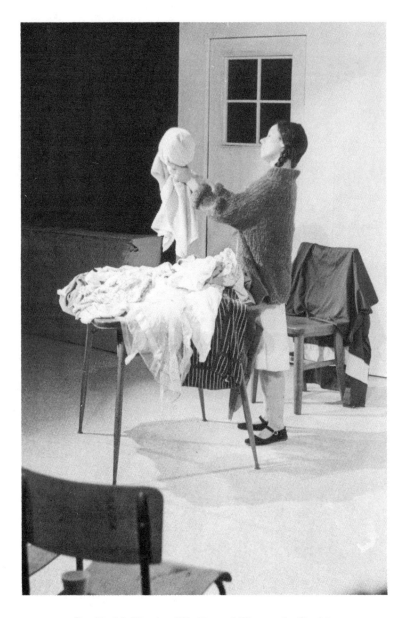

Sandie McGinnis of Driftwood Players in *Sophie*
February, 1987

Sophie

Cast:

One woman   One voice

Production Notes

I doubt if there is anyone alive who has not at some time felt the urge to kill someone. For a brief moment, just the mere thought of actually eliminating a rival or a menace in our lives in a complete and final fashion can sometimes buoy us up enough to feel that the problem is at least temporarily solved. The thought is enough, the act itself unnecessary.

For a relatively few desperate people the urge to kill must be acted out completely. For others, such as Sophie, a symbolic act will suffice.

She is simply a girl harassed by an unseen person. The harassment is obviously not new; Sophie's attitude tells us that the voice is omnipresent. But is the voice that of a real person — perhaps a parent or employer — or is the voice disembodied? Is Sophie "hearing things"? Is she the victim of hallucinations?

The director and actors must decide the relationship between Sophie and the voice to their own satisfaction. Then the problem of how to present the voice is half solved. Three suggestions are given in the playscript; there are many more possibilities.

The actor playing Sophie must remember to keep the histrionics in check, concentrating on the construction of the "body". Only in her final actions is Sophie overtly destructive, and the audience must be left wondering if, at some later date, Sophie will require more than a symbolic murder to gain final satisfaction.

The actor playing the voice must concentrate on maintaining an abrasive quality so that the sympathy of the audience is held by Sophie up to the very last moment.

This playlet is a problem in "focus". The actor playing Sophie must hold the attention of the audience so that they are not constantly searching for the source of the voice. If the focus leaves Sophie, the audience will not follow the plot, simple though it is. The following basic exercises in "concentration" will help the actors.

Preparation:

1. a) Pile an invisible stack of childrens' building blocks carefully one by one on top of each other. The actor must see the size and the shape of the blocks to align them properly.

   b) Knock the stack down and repeat the exercise in front of an audience of one or two persons who will criticize the inaccuracies of the performance.

2. a) Put a diaper on an invisible child, prepare his food and feed him.

   b) Repeat the process, stopping after each completed action to analyze the moves made. Decide which moves are superfluous. Concentrate only on the actions which convey the message. Make these actions precise.

   c) Repeat the performance for an audience of classmates.

   For more practice in the precise manipulation of stage properties try *Sculpture with Invisible Clay* (Workshop 3).

Sophie

Scene: A table and a chair on a bare stage. SOPHIE stands beside the table folding a great pile of sheets, pillowcases, towels, tea towels, washcloths, and tablecloths. SOPHIE's age is indefinite, her clothing unremarkable. The actor playing the part must avoid playing the "message". SOPHIE's relationship to the voice must be decided by the actor, but in all events she must be played simply, without exaggerated facial expressions or gestures.

The voice of the unseen character is abrasive, sexless, ageless. It may be handled in one or all of three ways: an offstage voice; an amplified "God" voice; or various voices spotted in the audience.

VOICE: The kettle's boiling.

SOPHIE: *(Shaking out a sheet)* **Yes.**

VOICE: *(After a pause)* **I said the kettle's boiling.**

SOPHIE: *(Folding sheet. She speaks a little louder but without rancour)* **Yes.**

VOICE: *(After a pause)* **Get the edges even.**

SOPHIE: **Yes.**

VOICE: **I said get the edges even.**

SOPHIE: *(Louder but still without rancour)* **Yes.** *(She lays the sheet on the table.)*

VOICE: *(After a pause)* **Wasting!**

SOPHIE: **Yes.** *(Picks up towel, shakes it out.)*

VOICE: **I said wasting!**

SOPHIE: *(Louder)* **Yes.** *(She balls up the towel between both hands slowly, her face betraying no change in emotion.)*

VOICE: **Wasting electricity.**

SOPHIE: **Yes.** *(She contemplates towel, reaches for another [pink] one. She stuffs the first one within the pink one, smooths it to form a ball, holding the surplus ends of the pink towel in her left hand. She holds the "head" so formed at arm's length.)*

1   **VOICE:**   **Wasting what?**

2   **SOPHIE:**   *(Patting the head and speaking calmly)* **Wasting**

3   **electricity.** *(She picks up tea towel, ties it tenderly around the*

4   *"neck" of the head as if it were a bowtie.)*

5   **VOICE:**   **Wasting electricity with that KETTLE!**

6   **SOPHIE:**   **Yes.** *(She lays the head on the sheet on the table. She*

7   *stuffs a white pillowcase with towels, and plumps the pillow.*

8   *When she can not find room for it on the table, with a single*

9   *gesture, she sweeps the remaining laundry onto the floor.)*

10   **VOICE:**   *(After a pause)* **I said wasting electricity with that**

11   **kettle.**

12   **SOPHIE:**   *(Quietly)* **Yes.** *(She rearranges the sheet; places a pillow*

13   *on sheet, and the head on the pillow. She admires her work, then*

14   *goes behind the table, picks up several towels, bunches them up*

15   *on the sheet to form a sort of "body".)*

16   **VOICE:**   **Boil all the water away.**

17   **SOPHIE:**   *(Facing the audience, forming the words, but emitting no*

18   *sound)* **I DON'T CARE.**

19   **VOICE:**   **What did you say?**

20   **SOPHIE:**   *(Closing her eyes in resignation for a moment, she sighs,*

21   *picks up another sheet, folds it in half once. Then speaking*

22   *calmly)* **I said I know.**

23   **VOICE:**   **You know what?** *(SOPHIE lays the sheet over the body,*

24   *tucks the sheet under the "chin" of the head.)*

25   **VOICE:**   **I said you know what?**

26   **SOPHIE:**   *(She smooths the "brow" of the figure in the "bed". Calmly)*

27   **I said I know what . . . you said.**

28   **VOICE:**   *(Triumphantly)* **What did I say?**

29   **SOPHIE:**   *(She adjusts the figure's bowtie; she pauses, both hands*

30   *on the tie. Then slowly, smilingly, she throttles the figure by*

31   *pulling on both ends of the tea towel, adding emphasis with her*

32   *words.)* **THE . . . KETTLE'S BOILING!** *(There is a long*

33   *silence; SOPHIE begins to giggle and puts her hand to her mouth*

34   *to suppress the noise, but the laughter escapes, building until it*

35   *is nearly hysteria.)*

1   **VOICE:**   **SOPHIE!** *(SOPHIE puts her hands to her mouth to cut off*
2   *her laughter; her eyes are terrified.)* **Are you making the tea?**
3   *(SOPHIE becomes calm, lowers her hands from her face. She*
4   *walks to the table and contemptuously sweeps the laundry "body"*
5   *to the floor).*
6   **SOPHIE:**   **Yes.**
7
8
9
10
11
12
13
14
15
16
17
18
19
20
21
22
23
24
25
26
27
28
29
30
31
32
33
34
35

The Victim

Cast:

One man   *One woman*

Production Notes

This play is an exercise in presenting relationships between people. Our attitudes to others are based on our experiences in previous relationships. Sometimes these experiences are consistently negative: We become less trusting in each succeeding encounter; we are less willing to take people at face value, more likely to make unfavorable comparisons with persons met in past encounters.

The Victim and the Abductor view each other in the light of their previous experiences. As long as the Victim believes his abductor is a man, he does not try to escape or to bargain. Why? He is the North American businessman who, having reached his forties without having achieved his own private office and "three secretaries" secretly recognizes himself to be a failure. For him, the Abductor has the same power over him as the company president; the gun is the symbol of authority. So he uses the routine that he usually employs at company social functions. He chatters nervously, makes overhearty jokes, awaits the boss's permission to sit, even blurts out his private life with embarrassing candor as if he were with "the boys".

When he decides that the Abductor is a woman, he changes the rules for the encounter. First, he tries the Mel Falhurst technique, but doesn't realize that Falhurst's success has been due to his more successful personal style and to the different type of female (that is, the social female) at which that style has been aimed. The Victim's approach is tactless and patronizing, calling the Abductor "baby" and "honey". When she knocks him down, he is forced to rethink again the rules of the encounter. As he has never met a woman before under these circumstances, he comes up with the next best set of pre-conditioning experiences, his relationship with his wife, Marian. As a result, he accepts the Abductor as a tough adversary but believes she can be bought. He offers her wealth and fancy clothes because Marian would quite happily sell her soul for these things. He has to rely on a set of stereotyped male-female relationships because he is the Victim of his own society.

The Abductor belongs to a guerilla group where the sex of the member has no bearing on assignments or responsibilities. She has obviously done guard duty in many a kidnapping and is prepared to cope with the Victim. It is almost certain, however, that she has never shot anyone before, at least not in a cold-blooded execution. Nevertheless, it is not because she is squeamish that she reneges on her instructions in the end, but rather because she pities him.

Preparations:

1. Invite the actors to sit with their eyes closed and listen carefully and analytically to the sounds around them. They must identify all of them, judging their distances and directions.

2. Go on a tour of odors. The actor is led to the sources of various odors for him to identify. Or items may be brought to him for identification by smell alone.

3. Have your actors observe the mannerisms of businessmen and executives, making a list of mannerisms and habits of those that they consider successful, and another of those they consider unsuccessful. From these choose one mannerism and try it out with the role of the Victim.

The most difficult staging problem in this sketch is the "combat". The actors might find an interesting solution to this by reverting to slow motion combat. It's a stylization trick, but very effective in such situations. (Try *Combat,* Workshop 8.)

1 **The Victim**
2
3 ***Time:*** The present
4 ***Scene:*** South America, where the kidnap of foreign businessmen
5 for ransom is no longer headline-making.
6 A bare room, with one wooden chair DRC, a door ULC, a
7 window UL; through the window a desolate mountain landscape.
8 ***Characters:*** THE VICTIM: In his forties; his business suit and
9 shirt indicate a certain prosperity. His clothing is now a little
10 rumpled, the knees of his pants dirty, his tie loosened. His shoes
11 are very dusty. He is blindfolded tightly with a white rag; his
12 right hand is bleeding from a cut across the knuckles.
13 THE ABDUCTOR: In her early thirties; dressed in
14 windbreaker, jeans and boots. She carries an army rifle. The
15 actress must not play her as a toughie, or as a caricature of a
16 women's libber; she is simply carrying out an assignment.
17 Neither her femaleness nor his maleness are factors in her
18 reactions to him; ultimately it is her compassion for him as a
19 victimized human being that is his salvation.
20 ***At Rise:*** The stage is empty. The door ULC opens and the VICTIM
21 is pushed into the room, followed by the ABDUCTOR.
22
23 **VICTIM: Easy now, fella, easy! Just remember I can't see!**
24 *(The ABDUCTOR shoves him forcibly with the gun butt. He*
25 *crashes into a wall, clutching at it to avoid falling. His automatic*
26 *response is to remove his blindfold. He stops with one hand on*
27 *the rag, sensing that there is a reaction behind him. There is:*
28 *the ABDUCTOR has raised the gun butt to club him.)* **No! It's**
29 **OK, fella, I won't touch the blindfold.** *(He lowers his hand*
30 *and begins to massage his wound gently.)* **I remembered. I**
31 **won't do it again ... Am I allowed to sit down? ... I'm**
32 **very tired ...** *(The ABDUCTOR lowers her rifle.)* **I'm not used**
33 **to all this walking. Fact is, I don't walk at all if I can help**
34 **it. Would you believe I don't even play golf? ...** *(His*
35 *monolog peters out; he turns his head in the direction he imagines*

1   *his guard to be.)* **Can I sit down ... please?** *(There is silence*
2   *while the ABDUCTOR studies him.)* **Just here with my back**
3   **against the wall ... for support ... Surely it can't hurt**
4   **if ...** *(With the gun butt she shoves him roughly in the direction*
5   *of the chair. He does not quite achieve its position, but realizing*
6   *that there must be some reason for the push, he gropes around*
7   *with his feet and kicks the chair. It topples over. He gropes now*
8   *with his hands, finds the chair, rights it, and sits down facing*
9   *Downstage.)* **Thanks ... thanks a lot.** *(He leans forward, his*
10   *elbows on his knees, hands dangling between his knees, head*
11   *drooping. A moment passes, a new thought strikes the VICTIM*
12   *and he raises his head.)* **Hey, are we alone? Just the two of**
13   **us? ... You're not supposed to answer me, are you? I just**
14   **meant ...** *(She becomes tense; there is a pause, then he relaxes*
15   *somewhat.)* **No, there's no one else, is there? You can feel**
16   **it when someone's watching you ... sort of sense it, can't**
17   **you? ... Yeah ...** *(His head droops again. She relaxes a little,*
18   *moves DL, sits on the floor facing DR; the VICTIM again raises*
19   *his head and turns in her direction.)* **Are you sitting on the**
20   **floor? ... This must be the only chair. Hey, does that mean**
21   **I'm considered company?** *(He laughs dryly. The ABDUCTOR*
22   *takes a cloth from her pocket, begins to polish her gun.)* **Ah, you**
23   **guys must get kinda tired too ... even if you're used to**
24   **the life.** *(He starts to droop again; then raises his hands towards*
25   *his face. The polishing ceases.)* **It's all right. I'm just going**
26   **to rest my head in my hands, see. I'm not going to touch**
27   **the blindfold. Just going to hold my ...** *(She rises to her*
28   *feet.)* **All right! It's OK, I won't! I'll keep my hands**
29   **down ... I'll rest my head here on the back of the chair,**
30   **OK?** *(He waits, senses there is no opposition, and adjusts his*
31   *position to rest his head. After a moment she sits again, and*
32   *resumes polishing.)* **What I said just now ... about being**
33   **alone ... was just because I wondered if someone was**
34   **going to interrogate me ... or something ... I wasn't**
35   **thinking about escape ... I don't even know where I am**

1   **anyhow. Oh sure, we're up in the hills! I thought we'd**
2   **never stop climbing.** *(Massaging his thigh muscles)* **I really**
3   **am out of condition, I guess, but . . . God, I'm beat!** *(There*
4   *is a long pause while he rolls his head wearily back and forth*
5   *on the chairback.)* **This is the first time I've been into the**
6   **hills in your country, you know. Marian and I were**
7   **always going to take a vacation at Lake Juerna but we**
8   **never managed it . . . Marian's my wife . . . but you know**
9   **that, I guess.** *(The ABDUCTOR is quite relaxed now; obviously*
10   *the pattern of the encounter is settling into familiar lines.)*
11   **Funny, you read about these things happening but it**
12   **always happens to the important guys . . . and I'M not**
13   **important! That's why I kept asking if you'd got the right**
14   **man . . . Remember in the truck I said . . .** *(He sits up; the*
15   *lack of a reply has become annoying.)* **Well, dammit, I'm not**
16   **IMPORTANT enough! I know you guys have made a**
17   **mistake! I'm just Joe Nobody at Tanasco Oil . . . damn**
18   **near a clerk! . . . Well, a little more than that . . . but a cost**
19   **accountant for chrisake! . . . You might as well have taken**
20   **the doorman! And my COUNTRY won't pay the kind of**
21   **money you guys ask. For a company president or an**
22   **ambassador maybe, but a cost accountant!** *(Leaning back)*
23   **Just ask my wife how low and despicable a cost**
24   **accountant is! She'll tell you . . . boy, she'll really tell you.**
25   *(Attempting a friendly sociable air)* **Hey, do you have a wife?**
26   **I'll bet you haven't in this kind of racket. No wife's going**
27   **to put up with the hours you guys must keep . . . but the**
28   **pay's all right, eh? . . . Or maybe the organization takes**
29   **all the loot and you guys just do the dirty work!** *(Becoming*
30   *rather loud and overhearty)* **As they say, let's hear it for**
31   **idealism! Everything for the cause, eh? Let's clean up on**
32   **the bad guys so us good guys can make it!** *(She is faintly*
33   *amused. His mood changes again, he sighs, rests his head on*
34   *the chairback. The ABDUCTOR takes out a package of cigarettes,*
35   *lights up. This business is complete at ". . . stupid thing to say".)*

1 I've never felt anything about my job . . . It's just a
2 job . . . . Marian says I haven't any drive . . . no guts, she
3 says . . . She's right . . . She is really right! **Mel Falhurst,**
4 **he started with Tanasco the same time I did; he's way up**
5 **there, three secretaries . . . Mel's her shining**
6 **example . . . Why can't you get ahead like Mel? she says.**
7 **Why don't you get a fat expense account like**
8 **Mel's?** . . . **Y'know, sometimes I wonder if there isn't**
9 **something going on there . . . Marian and good old . . . No,**
10 **that's a stupid thing to say.** *(He sits up.)* **Hey, what about**
11 **a cigarette for me, too?** . . . **I haven't had one since**
12 **breakfast and you guys cleaned out my**
13 **pockets . . . please?** *(The ABDUCTOR studies him for a*
14 *moment, decides he is now relatively harmless, and relents. She*
15 *rises, tucks her rifle under one arm, and approaches him with*
16 *the pack extended. She touches his hand with the pack. He gropes*
17 *for it, grabbing her hand. He takes a cigarette, still holding her*
18 *hand and the pack. Suddenly his hand moves up to her wrist,*
19 *and then he becomes quite still. Exploding)* **You're not a man!**
20 **You're a girl, for chrisake! Just a girl!** *(Alarmed and angry,*
21 *she pulls away, backing off to DR. He raises a hand to his*
22 *blindfold.)*
23 ABDUCTOR: **Stop, or I'll have to shoot you!**
24 VICTIM: *(Amused)* **Oka-a-ay, baby, I believe you! I'll behave!**
25 *(He stands up.)* **But listen, honey, can't we be a little**
26 **friendlier?**
27 ABDUCTOR: **Sit down!** *(She replaces the cigarette pack in her*
28 *pocket.)*
29 VICTIM: *(Waving his cigarette)* **Come on now, how about a light**
30 **for this thing, honey?**
31 ABDUCTOR: **SIT DOWN!**
32 VICTIM: *(Moving towards her voice)* **Ah, come on now** . . . *(She*
33 *hits him in the stomach with the rifle butt. He falls backwards,*
34 *toppling the chair, his cigarette flying. He groans, arms across*
35 *his stomach, rolling on the floor. She walks to the window and*

looks out. Gradually he becomes capable of speech again.) **What'd you do that for? I'm defenseless, dammit! . . . You've got the gun!** *(He sits up.)* **Listen, I know we can come to some kind of agreement . . . Hey? . . . I mean, there must be things you'd like to have for yourself, right? I bet you'd like some fancy clothes, eh? . . . perfume, jewelry?** *(He feels for the chair; she kicks it out of his reach.)* **Come on now, don't be like that! I'm trying to help you.** *(She laughs harshly.)* **All right, so I'm trying to help myself, too . . . But look, this is no life for a girl. . . You're probably just doing this cause there's no other way of making it in this country. But listen, I've got an idea. You get what you want out of it and I get what I want.** *(She watches him suspiciously.)* **That guy I was talking about, Mel Falhurst, now he's worth a fortune, and the company would really pay to get him back. You'll never get a nickel from them for me, but with Mel the sky's the limit! And I'll help you get him . . . I'm not asking for a share of the loot . . . that's all yours . . . all you have to do is make sure he doesn't come back!** *(She smiles at him with pity, shaking her head.)* **Well, how about it? . . . Come on . . . Baby, it's a good deal! I cut out all the risks, and you get all the dough.** *(She starts to laugh.)* **Now don't be a dummy, this'll give you everything you've ever . . .**
(Sound Effect: Helicopter engine fading in.)
VICTIM: **What's that? It's sound like an engine!** *(The ABDUCTOR goes to the window UL.)* **That's a helicopter! . . . that's right, isn't it?** *(The ABDUCTOR ignores him. The noise indicates that the helicopter has landed close by. The ABDUCTOR leaves through the door ULC under cover of the engine noise. The VICTIM shouting above the engine sounds)* **Is this the big brass arriving? Are you taking me somewhere else! . . . Is someone else here? . . . For chrisake, what's happening?** *(The ABDUCTOR returns with a photo in her hand, comes close to the VICTIM and studies him.*

1   *She puts the photo in her pocket, releases the safety catch on the*
2   *rifle, and points it at his head. Slowly she lowers the gun again,*
3   *returns to the door, closes it, then raises the rifle and shoots just*
4   *behind the VICTIM. He leaps to his feet, terrified, clawing at his*
5   *blindfold. She clubs him on the back of the head with the rifle*
6   *butt. He slumps to the floor. She walks back to the door, then*
7   *turns to look back at him. After a moment, she returns to him,*
8   *bends down to check his pulse. Then she takes out her cigarettes*
9   *and matches and places them in his outstretched limp hand.*
10   *After a moment she rises again and exits without looking back.)*
11   *(Sound Effect: Helicopter engine increases, then fades in the*
12   *distance.)*
13
14
15
16
17
18
19
20
21
22
23
24
25
26
27
28
29
30
31
32
33
34
35

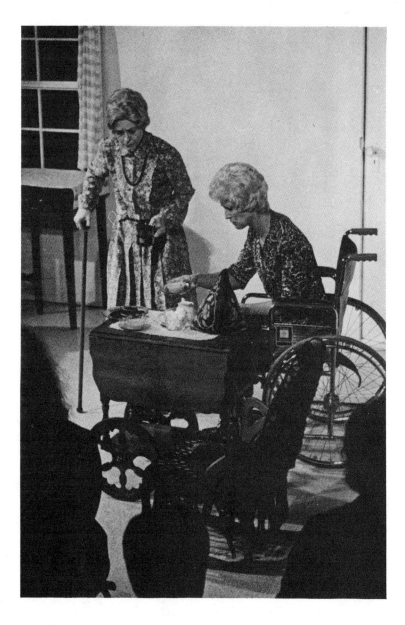

Fran Burnside and Sandie McGinnis of Driftwood Players
in *Tea Party* February 1987

Tea Party

Cast:

Two women   One boy (walk-on)

Production Notes

One of the techniques that actors must consciously acquire is the ability to use only as much tension as is required for the specific actions or non-actions that they must perform, to expend no more effort than is needed for a given situation. It is not simply a matter of economy. The "tense" actor is the one who cannot relax his *extra* muscle tension. Like the hunter who prepares an elephant gun to shoot a mouse, he's going to make an awful mess and completely obliterate his target.

In this sketch, the effort needed to perform the actions is minimal. The ladies' activities are limited, they are in the security of their home environment and thus have little fear of outside menaces; there are no violent passions here. Neither one is the quavering-voiced, palsied stereotype of old age. Theirs are more subtle characterizations. Alma has a cane and walks slowly, but she is alert and organized. Hester is in a wheelchair; the actors must decide exactly what keeps her there. She has considerable pain, which makes her somewhat more sharp-tongued than her sister, and of the two, her voice and actions would be a trifle more tense. Still, no marked tension or laborious effort to walk or move must be perceptible in either actor.

Preparation: Exercises for relieving muscular tension:

1. Lie on floor in a relaxed position. Slowly begin tensing, rolling the body up tightly like a pickled-herring rollmop. Slowly unwind, gradually returning to the first position and relaxation. Repeat several times, becoming aware of each part of the body as it experiences the changes from tension to relaxation.

2. Follow the above procedure, but this time, *spring* out of the rolled-up position and then deliberately relax. Repeat.

3. Stand, extending the body upward as far as possible. Then, without bending, shrink the body as small as possible. Return to normal size and relax. Repeat.

This sketch also presents blocking problems. Hester does

not move. It might have been established long ago that propelling her own chair caused traffic problems in the small house; or it could be that arthritic hands prevent her doing so. Alma does all the fetching and carrying in the house, so it is up to this actor to keep the stage balance. However, she must not wander aimlessly. She has served tea many times in the same manner; her actions therefore must appear practiced and purposeful, even a touch ritualistic.

Use the improvisation called *Old Folks' Home* (Workshop 21). Concentrate on developing purposeful routines and motivated actions for the elderly people involved.

Tea Party

Scene: The sitting room of the Evans sisters' home. The door to the street is on the rear wall UL, a large window faces the street UC. On the right wall is the door to the kitchen; on the left, a door to the remainder of the house. DL is an easy chair, UR a sofa, DR a tea trolley. The room is crowded with the knickknacks gathered by its inhabitants in three-quarters of a century of living.

Characters: ALMA EVANS: 75-years-old, small and spare framed. Her clothing is simple but not outdated, her gray hair cut short and neat. She walks with the aid of a cane, although she would not be classed as a cripple.

HESTER EVANS: 79-years-old. There is little to distinguish her physically from her sister, except perhaps a face a little more pinched and pain-worn. She sits in a wheelchair; but although her legs may be crippled, her mind certainly is not.

THE BOY: in his early teens, seen only fleetingly.

At Rise: ALMA is positioning HESTER's wheelchair UL. ALMA's cane is on HESTER's lap.

HESTER: That's it. *(ALMA takes her cane from HESTER. They both survey the room.)*

ALMA: I think I'll sit on the sofa ... at the far end.

HESTER: Yes. That will be cozy. Then he can sit on this end between us. *(ALMA sits on the DR end of the sofa. They both study the effect.)*

ALMA: But then he's too close to the door, Hester! *(HESTER nods, absorbed in the problem.)*

ALMA: *(Moving to the UL end of sofa)* Then I'd better sit here.

HESTER: But now he's too far away from me, Alma. *(ALMA stands; both of them study the room again.)*

ALMA: But if I push the tea trolley in front of you, he'll have to come to you, won't he?

HESTER: Oh, all right, Alma. You're sure it's today?

1   **ALMA:**   *(Pushing the tea trolley laden with cups and napkins, etc.*
2   *to HESTER)* **The first Thursday of the month.**
3   **HESTER:**   **You haven't forgotten the chocolate biscuits?**
4   **ALMA:**   **No, dear, they're on the plate. I'll bring them in with**
5   **the tea.** *(Goes to the window, peering up the street to the R.)*
6   **HESTER:**   **And cocoa?**
7   **ALMA:**   **I remembered.**
8   **HESTER:**   **You didn't remember for Charlie's visit.**
9   **ALMA:**   **Charlie drinks tea, Hester. I didn't make cocoa for**
10   **him because he drinks tea.**
11   **HESTER:**   **Oh. He didn't stay last time anyway.**
12   **ALMA:**   **It was a busy day ...**
13   **HESTER:**   **Rushing in and out like that. I was going to tell**
14   **him about father and the "Bainbridge" ... and he didn't**
15   **stay.**
16   **ALMA:**   **What about the "Bainbridge"?**
17   **HESTER:**   **Her maiden voyage out of Liverpool ... when**
18   **father was gone three months and we thought he'd gone**
19   **down with her.**
20   **ALMA:**   **That wasn't the "Bainbridge".**
21   **HESTER:**   **Yes, it was. It was the "Bainbridge". I remember**
22   **standing on the dock in the snow when she finally came**
23   **in. That was the year I'd begun first form, and I could**
24   **spell out the letters on her side.**
25   **ALMA:**   **It was her sister ship, the "Heddingham".**
26   **HESTER:**   **The "Bainbridge". You were too young to**
27   **remember. Let's see, the year was ...**
28   **ALMA:**   **Mother often told the story. It was the "Heddingham"**
29   **and her engine broke down off Cape Wrath beyond the**
30   **Hebrides.**
31   **HESTER:**   **It was 1902 and you were just four years old.**
32   **ALMA:**   **The "Heddingham", and she limped into port on**
33   **January the fifth.**
34   **HESTER:**   **January the fourth just after nine in the morning,**
35   **and we stood in the snow and watched the "Bainbridge"**

1   nudge the pier, and I cried and the tears froze on my
2   cheeks.
3   ALMA: The "Heddingham".
4   HESTER: Alma, mother didn't cry, you know. I don't think
5   she ever cried. My memory of names and places is sharp
6   so that I don't confuse them as some others I could
7   mention, but sometimes I can't remember things like how
8   people reacted. But I remember that day. There were
9   tears frozen on my cheeks but mother didn't cry.
10   ALMA: *(Nodding)* She said he didn't offer a word of
11   explanation. Just marched home beside her.
12   HESTER: *(Smiling)* He never did say much ... Is he coming
13   yet?
14   ALMA: No, can't be much longer though. Almost half past
15   four.
16   HESTER: Perhaps you'd better bring in the tea. Then it will
17   seem natural.
18   ALMA: Yes dear, I know. *(Exits out door UR.)* Everything's ready.
19   HESTER: What will you talk about?
20   ALMA: *(Re-entering   with   the   teapot)* I   thought
21   perhaps ... *(Carefully putting down the teapot)* ... perhaps
22   brother George!
23   HESTER: And the torpedo? No, Alma, he's not old enough
24   for that story!
25   ALMA: He's old enough to know about courage. I thought
26   I'd show him the medal, too. *(She goes to the window, peers*
27   *both ways worriedly, then carries on towards the kitchen.)*
28   HESTER: Not yet? He's late tonight. You're sure it's today?
29   ALMA: He'll come. It's the first Thursday. *(Exit.)*
30   HESTER: You have his money?
31   ALMA: *(Returning with the plate of biscuits)* I've got a twenty
32   dollar bill, Hester.
33   HESTER: Alma!
34   ALMA: Well, we haven't used that one on him. It was Dennis,
35   the last one, who always had change. We could get two

1   visits this way, Hester.

2   HESTER: Maybe Dennis warned him to carry change for a

3   twenty.

4   ALMA: It seemed worth a try. *(Goes to the window again.)* **Are**

5   you going to tell him about the "Heddingham"?

6   HESTER: The "Bainbridge". Maybe . . . or maybe I'll tell him

7   about the day the Great War ended. Remember, Alma,

8   all the noise, the paper streamers . . .

9   ALMA: And father sitting silent in his chair.

10   HESTER: It wasn't the same for him with George gone. Is

11   he coming yet?

12   ALMA: No dear, maybe he's stopped to talk somewhere.

13   *(Looking to the right)* . . . No . . . no, there he is, on the Davis'

14   porch now!

15   HESTER: I'll pour then. You get the cocoa, Alma.

16   ALMA: *(Going out)* It's all ready, I just have to add hot water.

17   HESTER: Don't forget the marshmallows!

18   ALMA: *(Reappearing)* Oh, Hester, what if he comes in and just

19   sits down closest to the door? He'll never stay!

20   HESTER: You'll have to prod him along. For goodness sakes,

21   Alma, get his cocoa! *(ALMA disappears.)* He must be nearly

22   here. He doesn't go to the Leschynskis, and the

23   Blackburns don't get home till after six.

24   ALMA: *(Returning with the cocoa)* Here we are! Just in . . . *(The*

25   *BOY passes the window. There is a slapping sound as the*

26   *newspaper lands on the porch. ALMA and HESTER look at the*

27   *door and wait, hoping to hear a knock, but they both know the*

28   *truth. Finally, ALMA goes to the door, opens it and looks down*

29   *at the newspaper.)*

30   ALMA: He's gone on by.

31   HESTER: You must have had the day wrong.

32   ALMA: No, he collected at the Davis'.

33   HESTER: *(After a long pause)* He couldn't have forgotten us.

34   ALMA: *(Still holding the cocoa, she turns from the door)* He's

35   collecting at the Kerighan's now. *(She closes the door and*

1   *stands forlornly.)*
2   **HESTER: Well, don't stand there with that cocoa! You look**
3   **silly.** *(ALMA brings the cocoa to the tea trolley.)* **Here's your**
4   **tea.** *(ALMA takes the cup, sits on the UL end of the sofa. There*
5   *is a long silence.)* **I think I'll save that story for the meter**
6   **man.**
7   **ALMA: The "Heddingham"?**
8   **HESTER: The "Bainbridge".**
9   **ALMA:** *(After a pause)* **They don't read the meters for two**
10 **more weeks.**
11   *SLOW BLACKOUT*
12
13
14
15
16
17
18
19
20
21
22
23
24
25
26
27
28
29
30
31
32
33
34
35

Winnifred and Grace

Cast:

Two women

Production Notes

Body rhythms are extremely important to the actor. She must decide the tempo of her character very early in her approach to the play. Simply reading the play aloud will help determine the speaking rhythm of each character. The physical rhythm must be developed from this.

In this sketch, Grace is much slower than Winnifred, her speech rhythms much more relaxed and flowing. The rhythm of her gestures and movements will match or complement this. Winnifred's speech is faster but also has a staccato, abrupt quality. It will, as a result, require much more muscular tension to present Winnifred than to present Grace.

The physical actions and handling of properties required by the actors are designed to express their emotions. (An actor, of course, cannot act an emotion directly; he can only act out its physical manifestation.) Thus, Winnifred's manner of handling the archaeological equipment and Grace's manipulation of her boots and her feet can be used effectively to express much emotion.

Preparation: Improvise situations in which properties are handled for specific purposes. Be aware of the rhythms involved.

1. a) Take off your boots because you have developed blisters on your feet after a long hike.

b) Take off shoes you have tried on in a shoe store. They're perfect, but too expensive for you.

c) Take off boots that you have just discovered to have been the property of a man who died of a communicable disease.

2. a) Handle a rock as if you're planning to murder someone with it.

b) Handle a rock as if you've just realized that it is gold-bearing.

c) Handle a rock as if you are a poor farmer with land strewn with boulders. This rock has just broken your plow.

You may also wish to use *Mirrors* (Workshop 6) to help establish rhythms.

The play's denouement should leave the audience guessing. Did Grace or Winnifred kill Philip? Did either of them kill him? Did their desire to kill him encourage them to take the blame (or credit) when he died accidentally in a fall? Did both of them kill him? Or are Winnifred and Grace just two halves of the same woman? The actors may well need a lengthy discussion period to make these decisions.

YOUR NOTES

Winnifred and Grace

Scene: An archeologist's camp. Upstage is a tent with mosquito netting sides and a door flap facing downstage. DRC is a camp table and behind it a camp stool. The table is piled with trays of specimens, bottles of fluid, small tools, clipboards, books and similar paraphernalia. On the ground beside the table are several large metal cases for specimens and tools.

Characters: Seated at the table and facing squarely to the audience is WINNIFRED: tan safari jacket, tan culottes, businesslike kneeboots, pith helmet. She is one of those rare women whose platinum hair is impeccably dressed even when months beyond a hairdresser, whose clothes are as immaculate as they were at purchase. She is intelligent and ambitious.

GRACE, her sister, who will enter shortly, is dressed in an almost identical fashion, but her clothing is slightly untidy (the scarf tucked into the neck of her jacket has come loose and is in danger of becoming detached; one bootlace is untied) and her hair is disarranged. Though neither prettier nor less sturdy than her sister, she gives the impression of dependence.

It is essential that both actresses avoid the stereotyped "tough" versus "helpless" characterizations easily available here. It is also easy to play both women as psychotics . . . resist the temptation!

At Rise: WINNIFRED is busy collating data on charts; from time to time she picks up a specimen of pottery from one of the trays, makes a few notes, returns the specimen to the tray. After a few moments GRACE enters DL; she pauses, watching WINNIFRED, then continues towards the tent door where she pauses to listen to WINNIFRED.

WINNIFRED: *(Without looking up, as GRACE crosses):* **Well, that's about it. The last item indexed from that final quadrant. Not that this last site yielded much that was new. Still, it certainly has proven the reliability of the**

1   **earlier specimens. Good solid documentation this. Not a**
2   **lingering doubt left. Not that I had any doubts.** *(GRACE*
3   *enters the tent; WINNIFRED raises her voice but continues her*
4   *work, stacking trays, sorting papers and tools.)* **Certainly will**
5   **set the department on its ear. No more raised eyebrows.**
6   **No more condescending smiles.** *(Pause as she stands.)*
7   **Thought I might apply for a Schoner Award, do a series**
8   **of lectures on the Kisawara Gorge culture. Illustrated**
9   **lectures. Not just slides. Actual specimens. And then, top**
10   **it off with the Kisawara palstave!** *(She reaches into a special*
11   *tray and picks up a uniquely shaped bronze axe-head. She*
12   *handles it reverently.)* **Beautiful! Perfect!**
13   **GRACE:**   *(Re-enters with camp stool, sits DL, begins to unlace her*
14   *boots):* **Should make an early start tomorrow.**
15   **WINNIFRED:**   **By eight hundred hours, I should think.**
16   *(Replaces the axe-head in its tray.)* **Problem getting the**
17   **bearers started that early, of course. But it's two full days'**
18   **march to base camp and there's increased baggage now.**
19   *(Pause)* **Short one man, too.** *(There is a pause; both women*
20   *continue their activities.)*
21   **GRACE:**   **We shall have to pack some ourselves.**
22   **WINNIFRED:**   **Sets a bad example to the natives.**
23   **But ... well ... yes, if necessary.** *(Pause)* **We could leave**
24   **Philip's kit behind. That would lighten the load.**
25   **GRACE:**   **Create a bad impression.** *(Pause)* **With the**
26   **department.**
27   **WINNIFRED:**   **Yes.** *(Pause)* **Could leave his clothing. Just pack**
28   **out his cameras, field glasses, guns, and such.**
29   **GRACE:**   *(After a long pause)* **Wonder what he took pictures**
30   **of?** *(Silence)*
31   **WINNIFRED:**   **Of course, guns and cameras do add a lot of**
32   **weight.** *(Silence)*
33   **GRACE:**   **Yes.** *(She takes off her boots, shakes each one out, while*
34   *WINNIFRED continues packing, placing the objects from the*
35   *table into the metal containers.)* **Handled a gun well. Most**

1   **people ... in the department ... would probably call him**
2   **an expert.**
3   **WINNIFRED:** No. *(Looks at GRACE.)* **Liked to create an**
4   **impression. Rather inept actually. Not quite the figure**
5   **he ...**
6   **GRACE:**   *(Firmly but not angrily)* **No.** *(She takes off one sock, begins*
7   *to massage her foot.)* **He did everything well. Sort of charged**
8   **into everything ... wanted things big ... fiery ... Used to**
9   **stand at the edge of the gorge at sunset. "Sunset red's**
10   **my color," he said.** *(Smiles)* **Poetic!**
11   **WINNIFRED:**   **Effeminate!** *(She enters the tent.)*
12   **GRACE:**   *(Still massaging)* **His hands were long ... delicate.**
13   *(Raises her hands to her cheeks and gently strokes them.)* **Very**
14   **soft ... cool ... c-oo-oool.**
15   **WINNIFRED:**   *(Returning with more cases, which she proceeds to*
16   *open, removing goods and re-packing them.)* **Cold! His hands**
17   **were cold ... like his mind! Cold and calculating. Unable**
18   **to accept defeat. Wanted to claim the Kisawara Gorge**
19   **Culture for himself! Could never accept it that I had**
20   **discovered the palstave that made it scientific fact!**
21   **GRACE:**   *(Quietly, hands still on her face)* **We discovered the**
22   **palstave.**
23   **WINNIFRED:**   *(After a pause)* **We discovered it.** *(Pause)* **I**
24   **discussed it with him that last night. I talked to him for**
25   **hours.** *(GRACE is no longer listening.)* **He just got that set**
26   **look on his face. Slimy, egotistical face. Just nodded at**
27   **everything I said and smiled. Condescending!** *(Slams lid*
28   *on the case and returns to the tent.)*
29   **GRACE:**   *(Taking off the other sock and massaging her foot)* **Always**
30   **smiled a lot. Such a sweet smile, rather far away ... and**
31   **cool.** *(Smiles remembering.)* **Always smiling, even when he**
32   **was lying ... to me. He kissed my fingers ... that**
33   **night ... and smiled ... so far away ... so far away ...**
34   **WINNIFRED:**   *(Emphatically, as she returns with surveying*
35   *equipment, stacking it with the containers)* **Far away and**

1   **condescending! Wanted all the glory!** *(She is no longer*
2   *speaking to GRACE.)* **All the power and glory. I couldn't**
3   **reason with him! Started walking away from me. I told**
4   **him he'd be sorry. Acting as if it was his right! I begged**
5   **him ... but he knew the department would believe him**
6   **first. I followed him ... He didn't make a sound**
7   **... falling down ... down ... Not a sound.**
8 **GRACE:** **Kissed each finger and ... told me ... that it had**
9   **been fun ... but ... I cried .... He didn't even turn**
10   **back .. just left me there ... crying .... Just a little**
11   **push .... Looked sort of blurred as he went**
12   **down ... blurred and quiet.**
13 **GRACE AND WINNIFRED** *(In unison, turning unseeingly towards*
14   *each other)* **I didn't really mean ...** *(It peters out. They are*
15   *silent, not really aware that the other spoke. Finally GRACE*
16   *stands, picks up her boots, socks and the stool.)*
17 **WINNIFRED:** *(Beside the table)* **The department will expect**
18   **some kind of memorial.**
19 **GRACE:** **Yes.** *(Pauses, thinking.)*
20 **WINNIFRED:** *(Beginning to fold her camp stool, she stops and*
21   *looks up)* **Could dedicate my next book ...** *(Stopping, sensing*
22   *that GRACE has an idea.)*
23 **GRACE:** **Let's rename the gorge after him.** *(WINNIFRED turns*
24   *to smile at GRACE as GRACE goes towards the tent door.)*
25
26
27
28
29
30
31
32
33
34
35

Mr. Excelsior

Cast:

Two men

Production Notes

In this sketch, the old man and the boy underestimate each other. Sonny, to the saw-sharpener, is just another kid and the old man prides himself on being able to teach kids "a thing or two". To the boy, the old man is just another mark.

The play is actually a study in actor concentration, an illustration of the rule that attention demands attention. The audience must see what the actor intends them to see. It is not necessary for Sonny to make an elaborate thing of his theft. His movements need not be large; he does not need to "demonstrate" that he is stealing the tools. His tight attention to his actions, however, will make them quite noticeable in relation to the other movements on stage. It is soon apparent that the old man is operating in a closed orbit; he gives an illustrated lecture but is not aware of the boy as an individual. His movements are relaxed but sure; he has given this lecture so many times before that he knows exactly where to put his hands on all his illustrations. His movements have economy as he works within his own little circle; the boy stands like an exclamation mark outside this circle.

The boy is much more tense than the old man, but he uses this tension to maintain his stillness, not his action. His slightest movement, therefore, becomes a focus for the audience. He must not wave the hacksaw around to show he is stealing it but the audience must recognize what he has done in order to appreciate the rest of his actions. His concentration on this action will demand their attention.

Preparation: Establishing a focus. Work with orchestral music that has more than one easily recognized instrument to follow. Actors are to work in pairs, moving the body freely to the music, each one gradually trying to follow the dictates of a single instrument or group of instruments. Now deliberately analyze the movements, and confine each actor to only those of a single type, all rounded for one, perhaps, and all angular for the other. Have the actors alternate, trying to make spectacular movement effects that will take the focus of the "scene" that they are involved in. First one, then the other will invent ways to capture an observer's interest. This will require discussion at first but gradually talk will be unnecessary as each freely "gives the scene" to his partner.

For further development of concentration, use *Delayed Action Mirrors* (Workshop 6).

YOUR NOTES

1 # Mr. Excelsior

2

3 **Scene:**   A dingy saw-sharpener's workshop on an alley. On a window

4   in reverse is "Excelsior Saw Sharpeners". The door to the alley

5   is DL.

6 **Characters:**   "MR. EXCELSIOR": about sixty, in coveralls,

7   mechanic's cap. He has his back to the audience ULC. He is

8   whistling as he operates a machine that sharpens a saw clamped

9   in a vise.

10   SONNY: About fourteen, in jeans, sweatshirt, and

11   carrying a newspaper bag on his shoulder.

12

13 **SONNY:**   *(In doorway DL)* **Hey, you sharpen saws?** *(MR.*

14   *EXCELSIOR turns his head, looks, returns to his work. SONNY*

15   *takes rusty saw out of his newspaper bag.)* **I got this saw here**

16   **that needs sharpening.** *(Advancing)* **It's kinda old,**

17   **but . . .** *(MR. EXCELSIOR very deliberately stops the machine,*

18   *wipes his hands on rag, reaches for the saw, turns it over carefully,*

19   *and examines its surfaces, handle, and teeth.)*

20 **MR. EXCELSIOR:**   **Kind of old?**

21 **SONNY:**   **Yeh, well, . . . it was my . . . dad's and . . .**

22 **MR. EXCELSIOR:**   **How old is your daddy?**

23 **SONNY:**   **Huh? What . . .**

24 **MR. EXCELSIOR:**   **What you been doing with this . . . cutting**

25   **concrete?**

26 **SONNY:**   *(Embarrassed)* **Oh! Well . . . can you sharpen it?**

27 **MR. EXCELSIOR:**   **You been cutting through nails with this**

28   **saw! Look you, there's teeth missing here and**

29   **here . . . and by God more teeth out here!**

30 **SONNY:**   **Well, I just . . .** *(He moves to the left of work bench, resting*

31   *his hand on the bench.)*

32 **MR. EXCELSIOR:**   **And rust! Look at that rust! Can't cut**

33   **nothing with a rusty saw. Slows you down, catches on**

34   **everything. But this saw's no good in the first place, of**

35   **course.**

1   SONNY: Oh. *(He begins to fiddle with a pair of pliers.)*
2   MR. EXCELSIOR: Cheap. **You don't get nothing in a saw if**
3   **you don't pay nothing for it. Not much good this one. See**
4   **these rivets. A good saw don't have rivets in the handle.**
5   **Has screws. See those saws over there?** *(SONNY looks*
6   *where MR. EXCELSIOR indicates, and then he idly picks up*
7   *the pliers.)* **Got screws in 'em. Real saws those are. No**
8   **rivets. And see here,** *(Tapping SONNY's saw)* **see where**
9   **the metal's blue by the teeth here? That's because this**
10   **stuff is real soft. They had to temper it to get it harder.**
11   **But look at this one.** *(Putting SONNY's saw on the bench, he*
12   *takes down a backsaw from the wall UR. As he does so, SONNY*
13   *examines the pliers closely.)* **This is a GOOD piece of steel.**
14   **Looked after, this one was. Fellow that owns this one**
15   **knows how to use it. Cuts right he does. Doesn't push his**
16   **saw. Doesn't put the pressure on. Let's the saw do the**
17   **cutting.** *(He illustrates with the saw in the air, then hands the*
18   *saw to SONNY to admire it. SONNY puts the pliers down*
19   *casually, and accepts the saw.)*
20   SONNY: **Yeh?**
21   MR. EXCELSIOR: **Now this carpenter guy comes in here a**
22   **couple of months ago. Said he'd been a carpenter for forty**
23   **years. Said I couldn't show him nothing about saws. He'd**
24   **been cutting for forty years! But he'd been cutting all**
25   **wrong. Could tell by his saws, you see. Teeth all snaggled**
26   **they were.** *(To illustrate, he picks up SONNY's saw from the*
27   *bench.)* **I showed him the proper way to saw. Wouldn't**
28   **listen to me. Been sawing for forty years he said. But he**
29   **come back. Two weeks later it was. And he said I was**
30   **right. He's been sawing wrong for forty years ... forty**
31   **years.** *(Pause)* **But you don't push, you see.** *(Illustrates again.*
32   *SONNY holds the backsaw below the level of the table.)* **No**
33   **pressure on the handle. Just let the saw do its job, eh?**
34   SONNY: **Yeah, sure.** *(MR. EXCELSIOR turns to put SONNY's*
35   *saw on the bench. He reaches for a loosely bound manual on a*

1   *wall shelf UR. SONNY drops the backsaw into his newsbag.)*
2 MR. EXCELSIOR: Now this here is my saw manual. You
3   know, each saw is different, got its own personality, and
4   they're all in this book. Tells the saw's temper, angles of
5   its teeth, everything. All I have to do is look up the maker
6   and I know just what wants doing with it. *(He returns the*
7   *book to the shelf. SONNY scans the objects on the workbench.)*
8   Got to treat your saws right you know. Treat 'em right and
9   they'll treat you right. Yessir, you treat 'em right and . . .
10 SONNY: Well, if you can't fix it . . .
11 MR. EXCELSIOR: . . . they'll treat you right. *(Looking over*
12   *offending saw again.)* Maybe . . . maybe not . . .
13 SONNY: *(Attempting to take the saw)* Then I guess I'd better . . .
14 MR. EXCELSIOR: Haven't said I can't yet.
15 SONNY: Well, maybe it ain't worth . . .
16 MR. EXCELSIOR: Leave it. Leave the saw here. I just
17   might . . .
18 SONNY: No, I'd better . . . *(Grabbing for the saw. MR.*
19   *EXCELSIOR deliberately turning, hangs SONNY's saw on the*
20   *wall UR. SONNY shrugs, picks up the pliers and drops them*
21   *into his bag.)*
22 MR. EXCELSIOR: Call back next week . . . say Wednesday . . . I'll
23   have something done with it by then.
24 SONNY: But maybe it'll cost too much.
25 MR. EXCELSIOR: We'll talk about that on Wednesday.
26 SONNY: OK . . . sure, thanks. *(He grins.)* Yeah, thanks a lot.
27   *(Exit. MR. EXCELSIOR watches him go, nodding and smiling*
28   *his approval of the lesson he has just delivered. Pursing his lips,*
29   *he returns to his work, whistling.)*
30
31
32
33
34
35

Bridgework

Cast:

Two men

Production Notes

It is apparent that Man No. 1 is a hobo or bum; however, he is not really complaining about his lot in life. He might get momentarily depressed by his circumstances, but he rises easily above them because of his simple pleasure in ordinary things. He throws the cigarette package over the railing and soon becomes enthralled with something that he sees when he peers over the railing after it. Does it land on something, some unexpected target? Does it miss some arbitrary point that he would have liked it to hit? Does it sink into the water in a peculiar manner? The director and the actors must decide for themselves, in order to motivate the actor.

In any case, he becomes absorbed in the game, finally whistling and laughing as he divests himself of all his garments. It is only the intervention of Man No. 2 which deflects his intent. In a subtle twist, Man No. 2 suggests to him that it is the *coat* that will remain behind, and that Man No. 1 himself will go over the railing.

Man No. 2 is not overtly evil; he is in fact, quite wholesome and honest in appearance. It is not until the final moments that the audience should become aware that he is just an unscrupulous opportunist.

Preparation: This play requires the exquisite precision of mime; the audience must not miss any detail in the process of Man No. 1's growing involvement in his game. The actor must also convey clearly to the audience his changing emotions as the process evolves. Precede script work with simple mime exercises, concentrating on precision of movement.

1. Buy cotton candy at a fair, become enmeshed in it as you eat it.

2. Walk your dog in the park; meet an acquaintance there, taking your immediate attention away from the dog.

3. Challenge an invisible bully to a fight.

This play involves a dialog in which two people misunderstand one another, either deliberately or accidentally. It is as if each one speaks a different language. In preparation for this, try the last variation in the section on *Instructing with Real Partners* (Workshop 9).

YOUR NOTES

Bridgework

3 ***Scene:*** A bridge, with a metal railing running UR to UL. Sound
4 of traffic, as if cars are continuously passing. The audience sees
5 the action as if they are seated in a vehicle that has stopped
6 for awhile in the process of crossing the span. They are,
7 therefore, in the midst of the traffic.

8 ***Characters:*** MAN NO. 1: elderly, rather destitute, but definitely
9 not depressed or suicidal. He is dressed in a shabby dress shirt,
10 wide cheap tie, suit jacket, pants from another suit, felt hat,
11 rather worn oxfords.

12 MAN NO. 2: young (perhaps eighteen or twenty), nothing
13 to indicate a distinct social strata, clothing ordinary and
14 nondescript. He looks wholesome and honest.

16 *Sound Effect:* A car horn bleats.

17 *(MAN NO. 1 walks briskly onstage UR, his hand following the*
18 *railing. He is whistling between his teeth in time to his steps.*
19 *He begins to look worried, stops whistling. He continues to walk*
20 *but it is now apparent that it is his left foot that is worrying him.*
21 *He stops Center Stage abruptly. He bends down, unties the left*
22 *shoe and removes it. There is a hole in his sock; he looks stricken;*
23 *he wiggles his toe, gazes at it mournfully. Slowly he eases down*
24 *onto the pavement to sit facing the audience. He wiggles his toe*
25 *again; shakes his head mournfully. He picks up his shoe, is going*
26 *to put it on, is stricken again as he sees that it has a hole in the*
27 *sole. He puts the shoe down. Pause. He takes up the other foot*
28 *in both hands, turns the sole up. Stricken again! It has a matching*
29 *hole! He puts the foot down slowly. Pause.)*

30 *Sound Effect:* A horn bleats as a car passes.

31 *(MAN NO. 1 becomes animated again. He feels in his pockets for a*
32 *cigarette pack, pulls it out, opens it eagerly. Stricken again; it is empty.*
33 *He shakes it upside down; it is still empty. Complete depression; he*
34 *drops the hand with the cigarette pack, the hand opens; the cigarette*
35 *pack topples onto the pavement. He sits slackjawed; leaning his head*

1   *against the railing he slowly rolls it from side to side.)*
2   Sound Effect: *A passing horn honks.*
3   *(MAN NO. 1 continues to roll head, ignoring horn.)*
4   Sound Effect: *Horn honks louder, repeatedly, insistently.*
5   *(MAN NO. 1 gathers himself together slowly, picks up his left*
6   *shoe, begins to limp off towards Stage L. He takes two steps.*
7   *Stops. Turns, looks back at the spot he had vacated. He returns,*
8   *picks up the cigarette pack, returns it to his pocket, takes two*
9   *steps to his left again, stops. Turns to look at the vacated spot;*
10 *pause, he is thinking. Feels for the cigarette packet in his pocket,*
11 *takes it out, studies it, studies the vacated spot, then the pack*
12 *again. He takes two steps back to the vacated spot, drops the*
13 *cigarette pack. Turns, two steps to the left again.)*
14 Sound Effect: *Truck horn: BRA-A-A-ACK!*
15 *(MAN NO. 1 stops, looks back at the pack, turns again to the*
16 *left, raises his foot.)*
17 Sound Effect: *Truck horn: bra-a-ack, BRA-A-A-ACK*
18 *(MAN NO. 1 replaces foot on the ground, looks back over his*
19 *shoulder at the package. He returns two steps, picks up the*
20 *package, faces the audience, is going to put the pack in his pocket*
21 *but pauses. Now he looks cautiously right, looks searchingly left,*
22 *then throws the pack over his shoulder, over the railing to*
23 *whatever is below the bridge. Looks right, looks left, turns left,*
24 *takes two steps. Pauses, thinking.)*
25 Sound Effect: *A car horn bleats.*
26 *(Galvanized into action by the horn, MAN NO. 1 returns backing*
27 *up two steps; with his back to the audience, he checks to the right*
28 *and then to the left, then looks over the railing. He leans far out,*
29 *searching the area below; satisfied, he turns to face the audience,*
30 *looks right, looks left, throws his left shoe over his shoulder, over*
31 *the railing to whatever is below the bridge. Looks right, looks*
32 *left, turns left; takes two steps.)*
33 Sound Effect: *A car horn begins to blow but ceases abruptly as*
34 *(MAN NO. 1 quickly reverses two steps. He checks left, checks*
35 *right, leans down and removes his right shoe, checks left, checks*

1   *right, and over the shoulder with the right shoe. He is speeding*
2   *up now. Checks right, turns left, takes one step.)*
3   *Sound Effect: A car horn bleats.*
4   *(MAN NO. 1 backs up, checks right, left, removes his hat, over*
5   *it goes, checks left, right, turns left, begins one step, but returns*
6   *to his starting position. Momentary pause.)*
7   *Sound Effect: A car horn bleats.*
8   *(MAN NO. 1 faces audience, checks right as he unfastens his*
9   *pants, checks left as he lets them drop to the ground, steps out*
10   *of them, up they go over his shoulder, checks right, turns left,*
11   *smiling. Brief pause, turns back to face audience, looks down at*
12   *his socks. Checks right as he peels off left sock, left as he peels*
13   *off right sock; socks go over the railing. Checks left, then right*
14   *without even turning his head. He begins to whistle-through his*
15   *teeth. With excited hands, he unties his tie, pulls it off, over it*
16   *goes. Now alternately laughing and whistling through his teeth,*
17   *he turns to peer over the railing. Next he begins to peel off his*
18   *jacket, in very high spirits. When his jacket is half off, MAN NO.*
19   *2 enters from Stage L, and stands close beside MAN NO. 1.)*
20   **MAN 2:** **Can I help?** *(MAN NO. 1 freezes in mid-action. MAN NO. 2*
21   *takes another step towards MAN NO. 1.)* **Can I hold your coat?**
22   **MAN 1:** *(Still frozen)* **That's not what you said. You said can I**
23   **help.**
24   **MAN 2:** **Yah. And then I said can I hold your coat?**
25   **MAN 1:** *(Turning to him violently)* **Whadya mean can you hold**
26   **my coat?**
27   **MAN 2:** **Like I said can I hold your coat for you?**
28   **MAN 1:** **Whatya wanta hold my coat for?**
29   **MAN 2:** *(Reasonably)* **I thought maybe you needed someone**
30   **to hold your coat for you.**
31   **MAN 1:** **Don't tell me what you thought. I know what you**
32   **thought.**
33   **MAN 2:** **Oh? What did I think?**
34   **MAN 1:** **I know what guys like you think.**
35   **MAN 2:** *(Offended)* **What do you mean "guys like me"?**

1 MAN 1: Just what I said. Guys like you. I know what guys
2   like you think like.
3 MAN 2: OK! So what do guys like me think like?
4 MAN 1: Guys like you think you'll hold my coat for me and
5   then you'll get to keep it.
6 MAN 2: *(Incredulously)* Keep your coat?
7 MAN 1: Yeah, keep my coat.
8 MAN 2: What would I want your coat for? I got a coat of my
9   own!
10 MAN 1: You're just saying that so I'll letcha hold my coat.
11 MAN 2: Saying what?
12 MAN 1: You're just saying that you've got a coat of your own
13   so you can walk off with my coat!
14 MAN 2: Look, I've got a very nice coat of my own and I'm
15   perfectly happy with it. *(Turns and starts to walk away in*
16   *the direction he came.)*
17 MAN 1: *(Calling after him)* Whatsa matter with my coat? *(MAN*
18   *NO. 2 stops, turns to look at MAN NO. 1.)*
19 MAN 2: Nothing's the matter with your coat, but I've got one
20   of my own, so I don't want it. Besides, it wouldn't even
21   fit me.
22 MAN 1: Whadya mean it wouldn't fit you? You tryna say
23   there's something wrong with my size?
24 MAN 2: No, I'm not trying to say that there is something
25   wrong with your size. I'm trying to say that your coat
26   wouldn't fit me.
27 MAN 1: *(Belligerently)* There's nothing wrong with my coat!
28 MAN 2: *(Coming back to MAN NO. 1)* All right. So there's
29   nothing wrong with your coat. It's a very nice coat.
30 MAN 1: Whydya say that?
31 MAN 2: Why did I say what?
32 MAN 1: Whydya say it's a very nice coat?
33 MAN 2: *(Exasperated)* I said it's a very nice coat because you
34   said there's nothing wrong with your coat.
35 MAN 1: So you think it's a very nice coat so you wanta walk

1   **off with it.**
2   **MAN 2:** *(Patiently)* **It's a very nice coat and there's nothing**
3   **wrong with it except that it wouldn't fit me! See, I'll show**
4   **you.** *(Attempts to take the coat.)*
5   **MAN 1:** *(Hugging the coat to himself)* **Leggo of my coat! I know**
6   **whacher up to!**
7   **MAN 2: OK, what am I up to?**
8   **MAN 1: You wanna hold my coat so you can walk off with it.**
9   **MAN 2:** *(Moaning in exasperation)* **Why should I want it if it**
10   **doesn't fit me?**
11   **MAN 1: Howdya know it doesn't fit you?**
12   **MAN 2:** *(As if to a child)* **I know because it looks like it wouldn't**
13   **fit me.** *(Turns as if to leave.)*
14   **MAN 1:** *(Raising his voice)* **You can't prove that!** *(MAN NO. 2*
15   *stops.)* **You haven't tried it on.**
16   **MAN 2:** *(Turns back)* **OK. I'll show you.** *(He attempts to take the*
17   *coat again.)*
18   **MAN 1:** *(Suspicious and uncertain)* **No.** *(Pauses, silently sizing up*
19   *his opponent.)* **I know whacher up to.**
20   **MAN 2:** *(With great patience)* **Look, you just said that I don't**
21   **know if it doesn't fit me if I haven't tried it on, and I'm**
22   **just trying to show you that it doesn't fit me by trying it**
23   **on, see?** *(Pause)*
24   **MAN 1:** *(Being won over in spite of his suspicions)* **You're sure**
25   **you don't want my coat?**
26   **MAN 2: What do I want with a coat that doesn't fit me?** *(Pause)*
27   **MAN 1: Awright, you can hold my coat.** *(MAN NO. 2 takes the*
28   *coat, holds it by the collar in one hand, the other hand on his*
29   *hip. He waits, looking unconcerned. MAN NO. 1 smiles, rubs*
30   *his hands together in anticipation, checks right, checks left, turns*
31   *his back on the audience, climbs the railing and jumps. There*
32   *is no sound. MAN NO. 2 casually checks right, checks left, turns,*
33   *leans over the railing, studying the terrain below. He turns to*
34   *face the audience, checks right, checks left, puts on the coat; it*
35   *fits perfects! He shows no surprise. He buttons up the coat,*

1   *and walks off Stage Right whistling through his teeth.)*
2   *Sound Effect: Truck horn: BRA-A-A-A-ACK!*
3
4
5
6
7
8
9
10
11
12
13
14
15
16
17
18
19
20
21
22
23
24
25
26
27
28
29
30
31
32
33
34
35

In the Middle of the Night

Cast:

One man   One boy

Production Notes

This play concerns the aftermath of a disaster. It is not essential that the actors determine exactly what has occurred to throw the two characters together. It is enough to know that the event was cataclysmic and has wiped out all that was familiar in their lives. It is unlikely that they knew each other before the disaster, but being the sole survivors enforces their interdependence.

Preparation: Try the improvisation *Disaster* (Workshop 20) for an investigation of reactions in such events.

Each character, for his own reasons, refuses to discuss the actual events of the disaster, preferring to ascribe it to folksy, almost mystical, causes. The involvement that each has in these fairy stories wipes out for a while the reality of the present. Both actors must concentrate totally on the stories in order to ensure the audience's involvement.

Preparation: Practicing story-telling.

1.   Begin with simple well-known children's stories, varying the voice pitch and pace. Next, practice pausing for emphasis, lowering the voice to a whisper for special effect.

2.   Now tell the same story with the hands alone, no spoken script. For a better understanding of this technique, try *Handplays* (Workshop 2).

3.   Combine the hand story with the spoken story, using each to embellish the other.

4.   Invent a new story, reversing the procedure, hand story first, script second.

There is almost no physical action in this script; it is purely an emotional teeter-totter. Leo tries to force fatherhood upon Gerry; Gerry tries to force manhood upon Leo. Neither will succeed. The actors must be aware at all times which one should have the upper hand at the moment. Discussion and analysis of the script should tell them which one is dominant and which one is dominated at each point in the script.

Preparation: It might help if the actors mark their scripts with symbols in the margin to remind them when they're winning or losing as they rehearse or learn their lines.

YOUR NOTES

In the Middle of the Night

The Time: Perhaps mid-autumn.

The Place: A desolate area centered by a small campfire. On either side of it is a worn, dirty sleeping bag, each one occupied by a motionless figure. Upstage of the fire are two pair of much-abused hiking boots, one large, one medium-small in size.

Characters: GERRY: in the right sleeping bag. A man of about sixty years, wiry, obviously used to roughing it. He is part prophet, part frontiersman, a bit of a ne'er-do-well and con man. His life before this time had been free, a constant progress from place to place, easy temporary friendships easily dismissed when he moved on again. Now, however, he is forced to depend on and encourage LEO's companionship because there is, literally, no other choice of company. He is dressed in heavy woolen clothing and a woolen cap with earflaps fastened up off his ears.

LEO: in the left sleeping bag. Appears to be ten or eleven years old, but his mind often reverts to that of a four year old, and sometimes has flashes of an adult cynicism. He is dressed in an Indian sweater and hat.

The relationship between these two indicates that they have been together for some time, and reveals varying degrees and kinds of love, tolerance of each other's weaknesses, and sometimes the seeds of a hatred born of compulsory interdependence.

At Rise: The sleeping bag at the left wobbles, its occupant stirring. The movement stops, and there is stillness again. The bag stirs again. Stillness again.

LEO: *(Whispering)* **Gerry?** *(Silence. The sleeping bag at the left wobbles; there are some grunts and snuffles, and LEO sits up. Whispers.)* **Gerry?** *(Silence, then whispers.)* **Are you awake?** *(Silence, then louder.)* **Gerry?**

GERRY: *(Without moving)* **M-m-mufff?**

1   **LEO:**   **Gerry, are you awake?**
2   **GERRY:**   **Nope.** *(He rearranges himself in his sleeping bag and*
3   *prepares to ignore LEO.)*
4   **LEO:**   **My feet are cold.**
5   **GERRY:**   **M-m-m-ufff.**
6   **LEO:**   **My feet are cold.**
7   **GERRY:**   *(After a colossal upheaval within the sleeping bag)* **What?**
8   **LEO:**   *(Loudly, carefully pronouncing every word)* **MY FEET ARE**
9   **COLD!**
10   **GERRY:**   *(After a pause)* **Put 'em in your pockets.** *(GERRY*
11   *resettles. LEO sits thinking for a while. Finally, he eases out of*
12   *his sleeping bag and sits on top of it. He reaches for one of the*
13   *smaller boots, changes his mind, puts it back, and reaches for*
14   *the bigger boots. He puts them on, lacing and tying them with*
15   *grunts of exertion. Finally the task is complete, and he stands*
16   *and takes several steps DL, the outsize boots clumping noisily.*
17   *He turns to see if GERRY is reacting; when there is no reaction,*
18   *he continues to clump DL, and GERRY raises himself on his*
19   *elbows to watch. Wearily.)* **What is it this time, Leo?** *(LEO*
20   *stops, refusing to look at GERRY. Finally he speaks.)*
21   **LEO:**   **I'm running away.**
22   **GERRY:**   *(Without apparent surprise)* **In the middle of the night?**
23   **LEO:**   **My feet are cold.**
24   **GERRY:**   **Oh.**
25   **LEO:**   **And I'm hungry.** *(There is a long pause. GERRY looks*
26   *straight ahead.)* **My feet are cold, so I'm hungry.**
27   **GERRY:**   **Your feet wouldn't get cold if you didn't wander**
28   **round in the middle of the night.**
29   **LEO:**   **My feet were cold before that . . . They were cold when**
30   **I was going to run away . . . yesterday.**
31   **GERRY:**   **But you didn't.**
32   **LEO:**   **No.**
33   **GERRY:**   **Well, if your feet weren't cold enough to run away,**
34   **they won't be cold enough to starve.** *(GERRY slides down*
35   *into his sleeping bag; LEO stands thinking for a minute.)*

1 LEO: They might be cold enough to run away tomorrow.
2 GERRY: Or cold enough to starve tomorrow.
3 LEO: I'll run away down the mountain till I meet a bear
4   and . . . I'll eat him!
5 GERRY: Or he'll eat you.
6 LEO: There aren't any bears left. *(GERRY does not reply.)* **Are**
7   **there, Gerry?**
8 GERRY: What?
9 LEO: Any bears left?
10 GERRY: No.
11 LEO: Or owls?
12 GERRY: *(Sitting up wearily)* **No.**
13 LEO: Or turtles? Or potato beetles, or . . .
14 GERRY: *(Using a western drawl and trying to make it into a game)*
15   **Well, pardner, that's what comes o' being the fastest guns**
16   **in the west! Ain't nary e'n a pertater beetle that could**
17   **outdraw either of us two-gun toughs in the end!**
18 LEO: *(Contemptuously)* **That's dumb!** *(Slowly, LEO returns to his*
19   *bedding and begins taking off his boots. GERRY begins to resettle*
20   *in his sleeping bag.)* **Gerry, tell me a story.**
21 GERRY: A story?
22 LEO: A bedtime story.
23 GERRY: You want a bedtime story?
24 LEO: Yeh.
25 GERRY: *(Sitting up again)* **In the middle of the night you want**
26   **a bedtime story?**
27 LEO: Yeh! My feet are cold.
28 GERRY: Your feet are cold so I gotta tell you a bedtime story
29   inamiddleathenight? *(For a long moment, LEO refuses to*
30   *answer, resuming the job of taking off the boots. He looks,*
31   *however, as if he might cry.)*
32 LEO: Gerry, are you mad at me?
33 GERRY: No, Leo.
34 LEO: *(After a pause)* **I was going to run away today.**
35 GERRY: You mean tonight.

1   **LEO:**   **No, today. Before tonight.**
2   **GERRY:**   **You mean yesterday?**
3   **LEO:**   **Yeh.** *(There is a long pause. GERRY looks straight ahead;*
4   *he knows that LEO will finish sooner or later. LEO puts the boots*
5   *back in place. GERRY yawns. LEO wipes his nose on his sleeve.)*
6   **I didn't though.**
7   **GERRY:**   **Oh.**
8   **LEO:**   **I didn't run away. I was going to, but I didn't.** *(Long*
9   *pause.)* **I was going to run right back down the mountains**
10   **and go right . . . Home!** *(He says "home" accusingly.)* **I was**
11   **going HOME!**
12   **GERRY:**   *(Flatly)* **But you didn't.**
13   **LEO:**   **Nope.**
14   **GERRY:**   **Why?** *(LEO doesn't reply.)* **Why Leo?** *(LEO slides down*
15   *into his bag and pulls the flap over his head.)* **Because your**
16   **home's not there anymore, is it, Leo? Nobody's there**
17   **anymore!** *(LEO is obviously crying now, the shape in the*
18   *sleeping bag heaving with sobs. GERRY looks defeated, and is*
19   *about to return to his bag but changes his mind. For a moment*
20   *he sits, staring into space. When he begins to speak, it is in an*
21   *"old-timer's" voice, like the voices of the old men who used to sit*
22   *yarning on the bench in front of the general store.)* **I tell you,**
23   **boy, I stood there in the middle of that field, the finest**
24   **field of barley ever grewed. The whiskers on that grain**
25   **tickled my chin, they did! Heads as big as your fist, boy,**
26   **big as your fist!** *(LEO stops sobbing, but doesn't reappear.)*
27   **And then that hot greedy wind come snaking in through**
28   **the field from the east, crying for a share of my grain,**
29   **and calling for the black storm clouds to come and help**
30   **her! I shouted at her! I yelled 'Get outa here! This is mine!'**
31   **But them black clouds kept coming and that wind rolled**
32   **like an old sow through my field.** *(LEO reappears, raising*
33   *himself on his elbows, wiping his eyes and nose on his sleeve.)*
34   **Didn't take no more'n five minutes, no more'n five little**
35   **minutes. All gone. Jest mud! When that hail started I jus'**

1   **set me down and put the tin pail I was carrying over my**
2   **head to protect myself and so's I wouldn't have to see**
3   **what they were doin' out there. But pretty soon I was up**
4   **to my armpits in mud, and my head felt like the day after**
5   **my birthday celebrations. Clangety, clangety, clang went**
6   **that hail on my tin roof, boy.** *(GERRY pauses; LEO sits up,*
7   *anxious that GERRY should finish the story.)* **Afterwards, I**
`   **jus' swam home in the mud, but it was all gone too, boy,**
)   **even . . . even Leo's kitchen table, . . . so then I jus' . . .**
10   LEO: It didn't happen that way! It wasn't hail!
11   GERRY: *(Mildly)* No?
12   LEO: No, Gerry! Tell it the other way. Tell it like it was fire!
13   GERRY: Nope. Better stir that fire a bit, Leo.
14   LEO: Please, Gerry? *(GERRY begins searching his bedding and*
15   *clothing and finally locates a cigarette; he leans over, stirs up*
16   *the fire and lights his cigarette from it. LEO watches, assuming*
17   *an expression of exaggerated disbelief. LEO is trying to force*
18   *GERRY to tell the story by giving him the lead-in.)* **You**
19   **promised me you'd quit smoking!** *(He waits; but GERRY*
20   *ignores him.)* **Ah, come on, Gerry, the fire story!**
21   GERRY: Nope. *(LEO looks as if he will cry again; GERRY relents,*
22   *grudgingly at first. His voice now ultra-feminine southern-belle,*
23   *as he daintily holds his cigarette.)* **Well, I know, I know, lover,**
24   **but . . .**
25   LEO: *(As if he has memorized his lines)* **After all the trouble you**
26   **caused! You sit there with that damn thing in your hand**
27   **and call me lover!**
28   GERRY: *(Correcting him)* **Darn thing.** *(Returning to southern-*
29   *belle voice)* **But, lover, I didn't mean no harm!**
30   LEO: Harm? All those people! And you didn't mean no harm!
31   GERRY: Lover!
32   LEO: *(Standing like an evangelical preacher, accusingly)* **It said**
33   **NO SMOKING. In great big letters, NO SMOKING!**
34   GERRY: Wrong, wrong, wrong, lover! It said "NO SMOKING
35   BETWEEN TEN P.M. AND SIX A.M." and I lit up at exactly

1   9:57 p.m., lover! I wasn't trying to break no rules! 9:57
2   p.m. exactly!

3 LEO: But you were careless, and the fire escaped! It escaped
4   from your little cigarette and sped across the carpet and
5   grew and grew and got sucked under the door and
6   pranced down the corridors and then climbed hand over
7   hand up the elevator shaft and burst from the roof in a
8   tower, screaming to the skies, setting the clouds on fire!
9   And the ... and the ... *(He falters unable to remember the*
10   *next line.)*

11 GERRY: *(Coaching)* And the clouds rained sparks and fire
12   that ...

13 LEO: ... that dripped and sprayed, and they splattered on
14   the roof of the city hall, and sizzled across the hot tar
15   paper roof of old Ma Colby's tar paper house,
16   and ... and ...

17 GERRY: Hissed in the gas tank of Jeff Norton's truck getting
18   a fill-up at Mike's Service, and smouldered in the dry
19   sawdust pile at the planer mill, and plunged into the
20   paint barrels at the paint factory ... till they all became
21   FIRE GEYSERS! ... licking higher and HIGHER ...

22 LEO: *(Whispering)* ... and higher till ... till ...

23 GERRY: ... till they licked up Leo's house, licked it all
24   up, ... right down to Leo's kitchen table ... *(Very quietly)*
25   And then they turned all the fire faucets off, and ... there
26   was nobody left ... except for Leo ... and Gerry.

27 LEO: *(After a long pause)* Maybe that was how it really
28   happened. Hey, Gerry? *(GERRY does not reply; he butts his*
29   *cigarette and disappears into his bedroll.)* The fire's going out.

30 GERRY: Better snuggle under, Leo.

31 LEO: Gerry?

32 GERRY: Yeh, Leo.

33 LEO: Will you tell me another bedtime story tomorrow
34   night?

35 GERRY: Nope. Tomorrow night's your turn.

1   **LEO:**   **But what if I run away tomorrow?**

2   **GERRY:**   *(After a pause)* **OK, Leo. Bring your rotten cold feet**

3   **over here!** *(LEO scampers out of his sleeping bag, and begins*

4   *burrowing in with GERRY as the fire goes out.)*

5

6

7

8

9

10

11

12

13

14

15

16

17

18

19

20

21

22

23

24

25

26

27

28

29

30

31

32

33

34

35

Trick Doors

Cast:

One woman   One man

Production Notes

Most young people, in a rebellious mood, have thought about leaving home. This thought is generally accompanied by another: "They'll miss me when I'm not here to push around." The idea usually passes as the family crisis that gave rise to it dissipates. Increasingly, however, the shoe is on the other foot. Parents, especially mothers, are leaving home and the responsibilities of family life. Such is apparently the case with Agnes.

But is leaving home what Agnes really wants to do? We know the answer to this by her speech on page 128. She really wants Harold to be nice to her. That, simply stated, is her goal throughout the play. Everything else that she says is simply a threat: "Harold, if you don't say you're sorry, I'll run away from home!"

How did Agnes arrive in this plight? From the script, we know certain facts about her. She has one son, Harold; her husband left her a number of years earlier; she owns a small house; she loves cats. But the actor must decide much more about her to explain her actions in this play.

How old is she?

How much education does she have?

Does she work? If so, where? Has she *ever* held a job?

Who pays for the groceries?

What was her relationship with her husband?

Does she have friends?

Is she religious? Will she be driven to suicide?

Where will she go when she leaves home? What kind of a job will she look for?

What other atrocities has Harold committed? How did

she react to them?

Why did she allow Harold to become super-dominant? Some single parents are obsessed with guilt, feeling responsible for depriving their children of a second parent. Is this part of Agnes' problem?

The answers to these questions will help the actor playing Agnes to decide what rhythm to use for her speech and actions. They will help fix pitch and tone of voice. More importantly, they will indicate what she is really thinking as she speaks — that is, the intention which lies beneath her words.

Preparation: Analyze the script to find the subtext, Agnes' real feelings beneath the words she speaks.

She asks: "Harold, dear? Have a good day? Everything fine at the bank? . . ."

But she means: "I must act normal, say and do the same things I always do. I must not let him know that anything has changed."

Try to chart the changes in her intentions throughout the play.

YOUR NOTES

1
2
Trick Doors

3 **Scene:** The hallway of a home. Three doors face the audience; the
4   door UR leads to the exterior, the door UC leads to AGNES'
5   bedroom, the door UL leads to the bathroom. DRC is a hall table
6   placed so that when AGNES uses it, she is Upstage of it. (The
7   back of the table is therefore Downstage.) Above it is a mirror.
8   (This need not be visible as we are made aware of it as AGNES
9   uses it, but it may be suggested by a frame through which the
10   audience sees AGNES.) On the table is a brown-paper wrapped
11   parcel that has arrived by mail.
12   After HAROLD's entrance, his radio plays from behind
13   the bathroom door throughout the rest of the sketch. The volume
14   of the radio should indicate to the audience that HAROLD would
15   have difficulty hearing any of AGNES' dialog.
16 **Characters:** AGNES: the mother, fiftyish, in an unstylish,
17   housewifey dress and sensible shoes. Her voice is hesitant, the
18   audible "feeler" of a creature accustomed to rebuffs and
19   humiliations. She knows no status but that of a doormat, and
20   although in this sketch she rebels, the actress must convey to
21   the audience that this rebellion will be short-lived.
22   HAROLD: the son, twentyish, a flacid package of pale
23   flesh, curly blond hair, a face that might have been handsome
24   if it were not softly-fleshed and weak-mouthed. He must not be
25   played in a limp-wristed manner, however, for he is at all times
26   vicious.
27 **At Rise:** The stage is empty. After a moment, AGNES appears in
28   the doorway UC. In her hands she holds a shoebox, the lid
29   tucked underneath the bottom of it; inside it is something wet,
30   furry, and inert. Her eyes are welling with tears. She carries
31   the box to the table DR, carefully removing the lid from the
32   bottom, gently placing the box on the table. Sadly she caresses
33   the thing in the box.
34 **AGNES:** *(Whispering)* **Bobo. Poor little Bobo!** *(Her hands shake,*
35   *the tears spill over; swallowing sobs and shaking her head in*

1   *unbearable anguish, she starts to put the lid on the box when*

2   *she hears a noise from UR. For a moment she panics, uncertain*

3   *what to do, then hurriedly placing the lid on the box, she exits*

4   *through the door UC and quietly closes the door. Almost*

5   *immediately HAROLD enters UR, a cigarette in one hand, a*

6   *transistor radio playing full-blast in the other. He kicks the door*

7   *shut, goes directly to the door UL, enters and slams the door.*

8   *The radio continues more quietly from behind the door.)*

9   *Sound Effect: lock turning*

10   *(AGNES re-opens the door UC sniffling and wiping her eyes;*

11   *she listens in the direction of the door UL, then emerges with*

12   *two old suitcases, staggering with them to the door UR, placing*

13   *them beside the door. She returns to the table, sadly caresses the*

14   *shoebox, then squaring her shoulders determinedly she picks up*

15   *the other package and takes it to the door UL, and listens.)*

16   **AGNES: Harold, you home? You in the bathroom, Honey?**

17   *Sound Effect: bathwater running full-tilt continuing under AGNES'*

18   *speech to "Actually of course, dear . . ."*

19   **AGNES: Harold, dear? Have a good day? Everything just fine**

20   **at the bank? There's a package for you from** *(Reading the*

21   *label)* **Lover Man Fragrances. Came in the morning mail.**

22   **Shall I open it for you? . . . Harold? . . .** *(When there is no*

23   *reply, she begins to unwrap it as she talks, from time to time*

24   *sniffling and rubbing her eyes and nose. The package contains*

25   *a bottle of purplish liquid, labeled LOVER MAN COLOGNE.)*

26   **Harold   honey,   your   Aunt   Margaret   phoned**

27   **today . . . from Montana, dear. Remember Aunt Margaret,**

28   **Harold, my eldest sister, the tall one with varicose veins?**

29   **Well, she phoned today, Harold, and she's very sick, dear!**

30   **She can't lift her head off the pillow, can't even lift a cup**

31   **she's so weak . . . Actually, of course dear, she didn't**

32   **phone me herself. It was actually her doctor who . . .**

33   **HAROLD:**   *(From within bathroom)* **For chrisake, this bathtub's**

34   **filthy! There's crap floating on the water! Cat hairs! That's**

35   **what it is! Right in my bathwater! Cat hairs! Wasting my**

1   **skin softener! You know what I pay for this stuff?**

2   *Sound Effect: under next speech, water draining and refilling.*

3   **AGNES:** *(Biting her lips to prevent a new wave of tears)* **... but it**

4   **was actually ... her next-door neighbor who phoned.**

5   **Poor dear Aunt Margaret couldn't even do that for**

6   **herself, had to have this neighbor lady do it for her.** *(Moves*

7   *to the table, opens the cologne, sniffs it, makes a face, puts it*

8   *down. She continues to the door UC; still talking she exits,*

9   *returning with a larger suitcase which she places outside the*

10   *door UR, concluding the task just before HAROLD interrupts*

11   *again.)* **Anyway, she's asked me to come and stay with**

12   **her, Harold. To look after her, you know. She can't do a**

13   **thing for herself, dear, not at thing. I said, of course, right**

14   **away dear, that I couldn't leave my boy all alone. But she**

15   **just insisted, Harold, just demanded that I come. She**

16   **said ...** *(Suddenly inspired)* **... she said that she'd cut you**

17   **out of her will if I didn't come! Well, I had to say I'd come**

18   **then, didn't I?** *(Pause)* **I couldn't say no to that, Harold,**

19   **could I? ... Cut you right out of her will she said! ... But**

20   **she really didn't mean any harm ... she was just**

21   **desperate for me to come. I know she loves you, Harold,**

22   **just like I do ...**

23   **HAROLD:** *(From within bathroom)* **Where's my incense burner?**

24   **Can't you ever leave my things where I put 'em?**

25   **AGNES:** **... just like I love you.** *(Raising her voice)* **Your**

26   **incense burner is in the cupboard, darling, just like**

27   **always. I promised Auntie that ...**

28   **HAROLD:** **What the hell's it doing in the cupboard? I don't**

29   **bathe in the cupboard, you stupid old bitch!**

30   **AGNES:** *(Blinking, confused, trying to keep her thread of dialog*

31   *going)* **Yes, dear. I promised Auntie that ...**

32   **HAROLD: Towels! Where's my towels? Gawdamit!**

33   **Where ... are ... my ... towels?**

34   **AGNES: Beside the ...**

35   **HAROLD: Towels, towels, you dull-witted cow!**

1   **AGNES:**   *(Raising her voice)* **Beside the tub, dear!**
2   **HAROLD:**   **Stupid cow!**
3   **AGNES:**   **Yes dear. I promised Auntie that I would come right**
4   **away.**
5   *Sound Effect: Thumping as HAROLD tries to kill a fly with a towel.*
6   **AGNES:**   *(Trying to ignore the sound)* **... right away. She was**
7   **pleased. I'm going to fly there, Harold. Now don't be**
8   **angry, dear! I know you hate me to waste money, and I'd**
9   **go by bus if I could, but time is ...**
10   **HAROLD:**   *(From within bathroom)* **Ya-a-ah-hg!**
11   **AGNES:**   **But Harold dear, Aunt Margaret ...**
12   **HAROLD:**   **Flies! Gawdam filthy germgut flies in my**
13   **bathroom! You're trying to kill me!**
14   **AGNES:**   **Yes, Harold. So I can't go by bus ...**
15   *Sound Effect: whacking sound*
16   **HAROLD:**   **Filthy beast!**
17   **AGNES:**   **... and get there on time, so I got a flight for**
18   **today ... just an hour from now. But your dinner's all**
19   **ready, dear, it's in the oven. I wouldn't forget my precious**
20   **boy's dinner. After all, you've been everything to me since**
21   **your father left, Harold. And I vowed then that I'd make**
22   **it up to you. After all, it wasn't your fault that he left. He**
23   **even said so himself. He said, Agnes, I'm not leaving you**
24   **because I don't like Harold. He's a really fine boy, he said.**
25   **He's a fine boy ... even if he has this thing about**
26   **cleanliness.**
27   *Sound Effect: water running*
28   **AGNES:**   **You see, he didn't mind this bathroom thing at all,**
29   **Harold, so you mustn't ever blame yourself ...**
30   **HAROLD:**   *(As water sound stops)* **For chrisake, this water's**
31   **cold! You stupid cow, where's my hot water! I'll freeze to**
32   **death in this!**
33   **AGNES:**   **Yes, Harold. So you mustn't ever blame yourself that**
34   **he left ...** *(Her voice drops to a whisper as she fights for control*
35   *of her emotions.)* **... because he actually said ... he**

1   said . . . he . . . No! No, he didn't say that, Harold . . . he

2   didn't say you're a fine boy. Actually he said . . . that boy

3   is . . . vulgar . . . and . . . and   gross . . . and . . . he . . . couldn't

4   possibly be flesh of my flesh and the only clean thing

5   about him is his flesh and it reminds me of . . . a putrifying

6   corpse! And then he left . . . He put on his cap and he

7   left . . . backwards . . . his   cap   was   backwards . . . He

8   looked so funny going down the street . . . like he was

9   coming and going at the same time . . . I kept thinking it

10   was some kind of magic trick . . . like maybe he was going

11   with his feet and coming back with his head and if I

12   closed my eyes for a moment, he'd be reversed . . .

13   *(Illustrating with her hands)* . . . going with his head and

14   coming back with his feet. So I closed my eyes . . . and he

15   was gone when I opened them. I guess it was a trick all

16   right . . . but not the right one . . . He really wasn't much

17   of a man . . . never successful in anything he

18   tried . . . never could seem to . . .

19   HAROLD: Gawdam! Gawdam! If you can't leave my stuff

20   alone, stay out of this bathroom! You've been using my

21   facecloth! There's toothpaste on my facecloth!

22   AGNES: No, Harold, no, I . . .

23   HAROLD: Filthy cow!

24   AGNES: Yes, Harold. I'm sorry, but . . . *(Her voice drops again.)*

25   No! No, that's not true. I didn't do that. I didn't. I can't

26   bear to touch your things because . . . because your father

27   was right . . . about your flesh. *(She shudders, then pulls*

28   *herself up, marches into her bedroom to return with two coats*

29   *and a hat.)* I'm going to be completely honest with you

30   now, Harold. I was going to let your find out for yourself,

31   but . . . well . . . now I'm going to tell you everything

32   before I go. *(She goes to the door UR, pushes out the suitcases,*

33   *and throws her coats on top of them. Then she stands before the*

34   *mirror, hat in hand.)* I'd like to be honest with

35   you . . . now . . . because . . . Harold? . . . I went to the

1   **lawyer's yesterday ... Mr. Fiedler, you know ... and ... and**
2   **I signed over the house to you ... It's not much of a house**
3   **but now it's all yours.** *(She puts on her hat, then rests her*
4   *hands on the shoebox, stroking it with growing agitation.)* **And**
5   **I'm not going to Aunt Margaret's, Harold. She didn't**
6   **phone like I told you. She's not sick ... I just made that**
7   **up. I'm running away! I just got a plane ticket for as far**
8   **as my money would take me.** *(Giggling)* **I'm running away**
9   **from home ... I don't even know where I'm going ... I'll**
10   **just run and run until ... maybe I'll find your father**
11   **somewhere out there ... and we'll keep running**
12   **together ... maybe ...** *(She opens the box, looks into it.)* **I'm**
13   **taking Bobo with me ... not all the way of course ... I**
14   **took a little money from the account to have him buried**
15   **properly ... at a cat cemetery ... They make it quite nice**
16   **in those places ... I'll tell them he got killed by a**
17   **dog ...** *(She strokes Bobo once more, puts the lid on the box,*
18   *tucks the box under her arm, looks toward the bathroom door,*
19   *replaces the box on the table. Now she begins to fiddle with the*
20   *bottle of cologne.)* **I always kept hoping you'd change,**
21   **Harold. Sometimes I was sure that one day you'd walk**
22   **out of that bathroom door really changed, really clean.**
23   **I'd close my eyes when you came out ... but you were**
24   **just the same. It wasn't until you ... until you ... you**
25   **drowned Bobo ... that I knew I had to run away ... Harold?**
26   **Harold, if ... if you could even say you're sorry ... if you**
27   **could ...**
28 **HAROLD:**   **For chrisake!**
29 **AGNES:**   *(Running to the bathroom door, the cologne in her hand.*
30   *Hopefully)* **Harold?**
31 **HAROLD:**   **I've washed my hair with your gawdam Bobo's**
32   **flea shampoo!**
33 *Sound Effect: Glass bottle shattering against the bathroom wall.*
34   *(AGNES turns from the door in tears; then she straightens, her*
35   *body shaking with sobs, tears rolling down her cheeks; she*

1   *unscrews the cap on the bottle, turns and pours the contents onto*
2   *the floor in the front of the door, a libation to the god in the*
3   *bathroom. Still crying, she drops the bottle, collects her boxed*
4   *cat, and exits UR.)*
5
6
7
8
9
10
11
12
13
14
15
16
17
18
19
20
21
22
23
24
25
26
27
28
29
30
31
32
33
34
35

Down on Your Knees!

Cast:

Two men   *One woman*

Production Notes

In this sketch, the thieves set the stage for the girl's entrance. Before she arrives they have characterized for the audience the former occupants of the house. The audience already knows Martha's circumstances before she speaks her first word.

Although Martha's father does not appear as a character, the actors must make the audience aware of his enormous influence on the proceedings. The thieves are taking advantage of his recent death to loot the house. The girl is taking advantage of it to act out her defiance.

Most young actors have experienced enough of their own rebellion against their parents' authority to enable them to accept Martha's motivation. Many will also recognize in Ab's reactions some feelings akin to their own power drives. Ab may not be exceptionally intelligent but he intuitively feels the potential in the situation. His own relationship with his mother and her religious fervor is recalled in the present situation. His desire for revenge for her persecution surfaces when he is able to force Martha to her knees. For him, Martha is his mother; for Martha, Ab becomes her father.

Baldwin, the pro who cased the job, is a less complicated though more intelligent man. Perhaps he is best described as having fewer hangups. The actor playing Baldwin will require less tension, a nice contrast with Ab.

The actors must remember that they cannot act an emotion directly. They can only convey it through physical actions. It is impossible to will oneself to act sad or happy whenever one wishes. But physical actions should express the actors' feelings. What actions would Ab and Martha use in the circumstances of this play? How will gestures express Martha's defiance and hurt, Ab's exultation in revenge?

Preparation: Perhaps the best preparation for this play is an improvised "mellerdrammer", proceeding from the basic plot of *Down on Your Knees* and improvising dialog. What are the stock gestures and actions in which our heroine would show her feelings? How would our villain react? In taking the actions to ludicrous extremes the actor soon learns what must be avoided, learning to pull in and tighten his performance, eliminating unnecessary gestures and facial exaggerations.

The plot of this play is irregular. The actors must find the high points, or subclimaxes and final climax, in order to pace it correctly, building and releasing tensions.

Preparation: For an understanding of this technique, try the activity *Sound Patterns,* Phases 1 to 3 (Workshop 10).

YOUR NOTES

Down on Your Knees!

Scene: A living room furnished with heavy old-fashioned walnut
or oak chests, tables, and chairs, several uncomfortable looking
upholstered seats, and a multitude of framed portraits and
religious mottos. DR the door leading to the hallway stands
partially open; its hinges are on the Downstage side and it opens
onstage. DL is an altar, ornately carved, topped with a lace
cloth and silver ornaments. UC is a fireplace, its mantel crowded
with clocks and ornate figurines. About the room are other silver
and china statues and vases so that the room has a depressingly
formal, almost Victorian character. Fading daylight filters into
the room between heavy drapes.

Characters: The Thieves: AB: A bald-headed man, short, thick-set,
in a dark windbreaker and jeans. He carries a gun, and is the
spokesman for the pair of thieves.

BALDWIN: Known as Baldy, a tall dark man, morose and
cautious, and little inclined to conversation. He wears a dark
woolen lumberman's jacket and jeans.

Both wear tennis shoes and cotton gloves.

The Girl: MARTHA DENBARD: About eighteen, by no
means beautiful, but her clothing is bright and stylish, and her
hairstyle becoming but a little overdone. She wears a cloak of
anger and defiance like battledress to shield her sense of
rejection and loss.

At Rise: The stage is empty, then the door DR is pushed further
open and AB appears, gun in hand; he looks over the room, then
pockets the gun and walks further into the room, talking to
someone in the hallway. The conversation is quiet, but no
excessive precautions are being taken against discovery.

AB: **Is this the last room?** *(Pauses to listen to a reply from
BALDWIN in the hallway.)* **Yeah, it'll make a pretty good
haul! You sure know how to pick 'em!**

BALDWIN: *(Entering with two large cloth bags, each partially filled*

1   *with odd-shaped articles.)* **It's dark in here.**

2   **AB:**   **Yeah, it's them drapes. Come on, let's get on with**

3   **it ... the place is creepy, ain't it?**

4   **BALDWIN:**   **Yeah.** *(Dropping the bags, he begins to pick up silver*

5   *articles and examine the hallmarks.)*

6   **AB:**   *(Pointing)* **Hey, that's a good looking pair of whadya**

7   **call'em ... uh ... cloisonne vases! Whatcha think, Baldy?**

8   *(Goes to the mantel and picks up a vase.)*

9   **BALDWIN:**   *(Pausing to squint at the vase)* **Imitation.**

10   **AB:**   **Ya sure? Could've fooled me!** *(Replaces vase.)*

11   **BALDWIN:**   *(Extending a silver candelabra to AB.)* **Here, take**

12   **this.** *(AB accepts it and places it carefully in one of the bags.)*

13   **AB:**   **I sure could do with a cigarette. I wonder if the old guy**

14   **smoked? Maybe there's a box of cigars around.** *(He begins*

15   *to prowl, opening drawers and cupboards. Suddenly he*

16   *straightens and turns to BALDWIN.)* **Hey, that's funny! I just**

17   **been thinking ... I ain't seen an ashtray in the whole**

18   **house! And the library didn't have a bar nor glasses ... and**

19   **there wasn't nothing like that anywhere else! Hey, Baldy,**

20   **didn't this guy drink or smoke neither?** *(BALDWIN nods.)*

21   **Hell, what did he do for kicks?** *(BALDWIN points to the*

22   *altar. AB is puzzled.)* **What's that?** *(BALDWIN folds his hands*

23   *as if in prayer.)* **You're kidding! An altar? You mean he was**

24   **real religious?** *(BALDWIN nods. AB goes to the altar, kneels*

25   *on the step, and folds his hands.)* **Get a look at this step! It's**

26   **all wore out!**

27   **BALDWIN:**   **Made his wife and kids kneel there. Every night.**

28   **AB:**   **Hell, no wonder his kids left home!** *(Rising from the step,*

29   *he seats himself in a chair.)* **My old lady was kinda like that,**

30   **y'know. We didn't have no altar, but she was always**

31   **dragging me off to church. She'd whack me over the head**

32   **to keep me marching down the street to that ...**

33   **BALDWIN:**   **Ab, we gotta move this stuff as soon as it's dark!**

34   **AB:**   *(Rising)* **Yeah, sure. What else you wanta take outa here?**

35   *(BALDWIN hands him an article; he stuffs it in a bag.)* **You**

1   **know, when I got too big for her to drag off to church,**
2   **she used to send the priest to talk at me.** **He'd come in**
3   **looking all** . . . *(BALDWIN freezes in the act of handing AB an*
4   *article. For a moment, AB is puzzled, then he freezes too. Slowly*
5   *both of their heads turn toward the door. There is the slight*
6   *sound of a key turning in a lock and then a door opening.*
7   *BALDWIN quietly replaces the article, AB picks up the bags,*
8   *and both move silently to take positions Downstage of the door*
9   *DR. A woman's footsteps are heard approaching. The door is*
10   *pushed wide open, concealing the thieves from the new arrival*
11   *but not from the audience. MARTHA DENBARD stands in the*
12   *doorway, looking frightened but defiant.)*
13 **MARTHA:** *(Whispering)* **Father!** *(AB and BALDWIN exchange*
14   *glances. MARTHA shouts.)* **Father!** *(She flicks on the light*
15   *switch. AB takes out his gun.)* **I'm here, father! Martha the**
16   **Wicked has returned to gloat over you!** *(She walks to the*
17   *center of the room, frightened but defiant.)* **I didn't go to your**
18   **funeral, father! I went out and bought a new dress**
19   **instead! And I had my hair done. How do you like it?** *(She*
20   *turns around showing it off.)* **Just your style, right?** *(Laughs)*
21   **Right, father? I'll bet that was some funeral** . . . **all those**
22   **pious old ladies from the church down on their knees,**
23   **wringing out phony tears. "Poor Mr. Denbard, dying all**
24   **alone! His wicked children leaving him to breathe his**
25   **last all by his little self!" But you weren't alone, were you**
26   **daddy, old boy? You still had your righteous indignation**
27   **for company!** *(She moves to the altar, stands in front of it with*
28   *arms upraised, derisively.)* **Down on your knees, Martha**
29   **Denbard! The Lord is watching you!** *(She whirls around.)*
30   **NO! No, I won't go down on my knees, father. I won't!**
31   **You can't make me do that ever again!** *(She pulls the cloth*
32   *off the altar and the altar ornaments crash to the floor.)* **You**
33   **remember that day, don't you, father? I said I wouldn't**
34   **pray, and I haven't! I won't kneel, father, for you or the**
35   **Lord! Years and years of praying to suit you!** *(She sits*

1	*in an armchair, looks around.)* **And all this stuff! This junk!**
2	**All part of your image!** *(She gropes in her handbag for*
3	*cigarettes and lighter.)* **I hated this house, you know . . . but**
4	**mostly I hated this room. This awful room!** *(She strikes a*
5	*flame but forgets to light a cigarette as she turns to look at the*
6	*fireplace.)* **At least when mother was alive, there used to**
7	**be flowers here and a fire in that fireplace. It wasn't so**
8	**bad then.** *(Her face softens remembering. She lights her*
9	*cigarette. Then her face hardens, she jumps to her feet inspired.)*
10	**That's what this room needs! A fire! A great roaring**
11	**bonfire, father! Right here in the middle of the room!** *(She*
12	*begins frantically building a pile of furniture in the center of the*
13	*room, laughing and chattering as she works.)* **We'll build a**
14	**funeral pyre for you, daddykins! How do you like that?**
15	**We'll smoke out your old ghost, and we'll fry your saintly**
16	**spirit! It'll be a private cremation party, just the two of**
17	**us! No little old saintly ladies crying, nobody down on**
18	**their knees a-praying!** *(She has arrived DRC to pick up a*
19	*chair and is facing R stage when AB and BALDWIN push the*
20	*door to close it and reveal themselves. There is dead silence while*
21	*AB points his gun at her and BALDWIN shakes his head*
22	*reprovingly. After a moment they begin to advance on her and*
23	*she backs up a few steps.)*
24	AB: **Hate to spoil your party, Martha.**
25	BALDWIN: **It'll hafta wait.**
26	AB: **Yeah. You can have it later, cause there's some stuff here**
27	**that we need.**
28	BALDWIN: **Mementoes.**
29	AB: *(Giggling)* **Yeah, mementoes. Afterwards ya can have the**
30	**biggest bonfire in town. After we're finished.**
31	MARTHA: *(Recovering from shock)* **What do you want?**
32	AB: **Like we said, mementoes!** *(He keeps his gun pointed at her*
33	*while BALDWIN quickly selects objects and stuffs them into the*
34	*bags.)*
35	MARTHA: *(Incredulously)* **You're thieves . . . burglars!** *(She*

1   *begins to laugh.)*
2 **AB:** **What's so funny?**
3 **MARTHA:** **You really want this junk? Take it ... take**
4   **everything! It's all yours!** *(She giggles helplessly.)*
5 **AB:** **Hurry up, Baldy, this dame's looney!**
6 **MARTHA:** **Don't forget that clock. You'll get a good price for**
7   **that.**
8 **AB:** **You shut up. Baldy's an expert. He knows what to take.**
9 **MARTHA:** **Some expert! He's leaving those cloisonne vases!**
10 **AB:** **Imitation!**
11 **MARTHA:** **They are not! They belonged to my mother, and ...**
12   *(She starts toward the fireplace; AB trips her and she sprawls*
13   *on the floor.)*
14 **AB:** **Stay there!**
15 **MARTHA:** **I was only ...**
16 **AB:** **Shut up!**
17 **BALDWIN:** **Let's go!** *(Exit DR with the bags.)*
18 **AB:** *(Motioning MARTHA to Stage L)* **Get over there!** *(She starts*
19   *to get up.)* **Stay down!** *(Enjoying himself now.)* **You can crawl**
20   **over there!** *(MARTHA crawls to the altar and remains on hands*
21   *and knees.)* **Put your hands up on that thing!**
22 **MARTHA:** **Look, I don't care what you take from ...**
23 **AB:** **Get your hands up there!** *(MARTHA rises to her knees and*
24   *places her hands against the altar.)* **Higher!** *(Her hands grope*
25   *for the top of the altar.)* **Now start counting! You can turn**
26   **around when you get to a hundred. Understand? If you**
27   **peek before then, I'll blow yer head off! Understand?**
28 **MARTHA:** **Yes, I understand ...**
29 **AB:** **Count!**
30 **MARTHA:** *(Slowly)* **One ... two ... three** *(AB exits DR)* **four ... five**
31   **... six ... seven ...** *(MARTHA begins to get giggly and gradually*
32   *it develops into hysterical laughter.)* **eight ... nine ... ten**
33   **... eleven ... twelve ... thirteen ... fourteen ... The Lord is**
34   **watching you, Martha ...** *(Her hands slide down the face of the*
35   *altar.)* **fifteen ... sixteen ...** *(She leans her cheek against the altar.)*

seventeen . . . eighteen . . . *(Tears roll down her cheeks.)* **Well, father . . . here I am again . . .**

GRADUAL BLACKOUT

Perfect Perley

Cast:

Two men

Production Notes

Most young people know that sickening feeling of loss and frustration when they have gratuitously destroyed their own chances to get something they badly wanted. Often, it is pride and immature arrogance that have denied them what they coveted, and the same pride and arrogance prevented them from pleading for reconsideration.

Lionel is in this position. He simply *has* to prove his superiority and when he does, he discovers that he's blown his chances. Only when he realizes that he is facing almost imminent death, does he begin to plead. But by then it's too late.

The actor must be careful that Lionel's characterization stays within bounds. If he becomes too effeminate, he loses all audience sympathy, so that they will be only too delighted with his impending demise. They should find him loathsome, but they must also find him pitiable in the end.

The actor playing Rhal might have fun using slightly robot-like movements and voice tricks in his characterization. This must not, of course, be taken to extremes or the character will lose proportion. The eccentricities should be just sufficient to suggest to the audience that he is non-human, but not so exaggerated that it would be impossible for Lionel not to be aware of them immediately.

Preparation: Improvise a scene between Lionel and his mother. An understanding of her character will help the actor playing Lionel. What kind of woman is she?

Improvise Rhal's interviews with other candidates. How would they differ from his interview with Lionel? Is Lionel the only washout? If so, how does this affect the actor playing Rhal? Should he be thinking as he speaks to Lionel: "Darn it, another washout!" or "What a perfectly strange earthling!"? Will Rhal tell the story of his encounter with Lionel to other candidates? To the rest of the Zondians? Is he mentally storing up a funny anecdote?

Preparation: In this sketch the fuschia silk pajamas epitomize Lionel's character; the briefcase, Rhal's character. Try Variation 2 in *Junk-Characters* (Workshop 22) for more exploration of the relationship between character and properties or costume. What other hand properties could be introduced that would help express character?

YOUR NOTES

Perfect Perley

3 **Scene:** A portion of a room furnished with an easy chair, a table,
4   and a large mirror. One wall has a window but the view is
5   comprised only of grey nothingness, as if smog presses against
6   the outside of the glass. A door on one wall leads to a passageway,
7   another door to a closet. Three or four suitcases are placed
8   around the room, open and mostly full of clothes. One of the
9   cases is on the chair, one on the table.

10 **Characters:** LIONEL PERLEY: a "golden-haired youth", of
11   eighteen or nineteen years, exceptionally mother-dominated
12   and super aware of his attributes, real or fantasized. He is
13   dressed only in an elegant dressing gown and slippers.

14   DELEGATE RHAL: in his earthly representation, a young
15   man of twenty, dressed in a sportshirt and slacks. He carries a
16   small thick attaché case, and, dangling around his neck ready
17   for use, is a small respirator, like a very sophisticated gasmask.

18 **At Rise:** LIONEL is in the closet, obviously looking for something
19   that he cannot locate. A number of articles of clothing come
20   flying into the room, with a steady stream of muttering and
21   profanity accompanying the blitz. Suddenly, the commotion
22   ceases.

24 **LIONEL:** *(Bellowing)* **Mother!** *(There is a pause while he waits*
25   *for a reply. Then he appears in the doorway of the closet,*
26   *bellowing.)* **MOTHER! Gawdamit! MOTHER!** *(He walks to*
27   *the other door, opens it.)* **Mother!** *(A few wisps of grey fog enter*
28   *the room. LIONEL begins to cough, closes the door and leans*
29   *against it coughing.)* **Damn fog! Where is that woman? I**
30   **can't leave without them!** *(He goes to the suitcase on the table,*
31   *and begins rummaging, then stops.)* **No! I know I didn't pack**
32   **them. They've got to be in the closet!** *(He returns to the*
33   *closet where the commotion begins again. There is a knock on*
34   *the other door. After a moment, the door opens and DELEGATE*
35   *RHAL enters, with his attaché case and his gasmask. He seems*

1	*surprised at the luggage in the room.)*
2	**RHAL:** Hello? Mr. Perley?
3	**LIONEL:** *(From closet)* **What?**
4	**RHAL:** Mr. Perley? I'm here to ...
5	**LIONEL:** No! Absolutely no interviews! My mother will hand
6	out press releases after the launching. *(Emerging from the*
7	*closet)* So just be on your way now!
8	**RHAL:** But Mr. Perley, I'm ...
9	**LIONEL:** And I'm very busy, as you can see! I haven't finished
10	packing and I can't find my fuschia silk pajamas and I'm
11	not heading for that launching without them.
12	**RHAL:** *(Pushing the case on the table over to make room for his*
13	*attaché case.)* **Mr. Perley, regarding that launching ...**
14	**LIONEL:** *(Placing a hand on the case to prevent RHAL opening it.)*
15	No interviews!
16	**RHAL:** Right! No interviews. *(LIONEL removes his hand.)*
17	However, I am surprised at all this luggage!
18	**LIONEL:** Well, you don't expect me to go naked, do you?
19	When I arrive on the planet Zond, I want them to see the
20	finest example of earthmanhood, not some refugee!
21	**RHAL:** Oh. But all these suitcases! There won't be room on
22	the rocket!
23	**LIONEL:** They'll make room all rightee for Lionel Perley, let
24	me tell you!
25	**RHAL:** That's your full name, is it? Lionel Perley? *(He opens*
26	*his case and takes out a legal file.)*
27	**LIONEL:** Lionel Mutchmore Perley. I was named after my
28	maternal grandfather, the famous geneticist Lionel
29	Genus Mutchmore!
30	**RHAL:** Oh. *(Checks an item in the file.)* **And your mother**
31	**was ...?**
32	**LIONEL:** IS! *(RHAL looks surprised, then a little disconcerted.)*
33	Mother isn't anything! Well, of course, she is my mother,
34	and that's been a full time career for her.
35	**RHAL:** And your fath ...

1   **LIONEL:**   **Don't ask about father! We don't talk about him!**
2   *(He goes to stand before mirror.)*
3   **RHAL:.**   **Yes.** *(Checks off another item in the file.)* **Now just for the**
4   **record, you have, of course, no physical defects?**
5   **LIONEL:**   **Defects? We are discussing Lionel Perley! Of course**
6   **I have no defects! I am PERFECT!** *(He laughs lightly.)*
7   **Mumsy calls me PERFECT PERLEY!**
8   **RHAL:**   **Then of course you have perfect teeth?**
9   **LIONEL:**   *(Coldly)* **Naturally!**
10   **RHAL:**   **And your eyes are blue?**
11   **LIONEL:**   **Ultramarine.**
12   **RHAL:**   **Hair brown.**
13   **LIONEL:**   **My hair is gold, not brown!**
14   **RHAL:**   **Strange! The computer calls it brown.**
15   **LIONEL:**   **What's this about computers? My hair is**
16   **gold . . . antique gold!**
17   **RHAL:**   *(Shrugs, checks off item in his file.)* **Well, Lionel, that**
18   **appears to be everything. I'll see you at the launch**
19   **platform in one hour.** *(Produces another gasmask-like*
20   *apparatus from his attaché case.)* **Here is your fogmask. Put**
21   **it on before leaving the room and don't remove it for any**
22   **reason until after launching.** *(He closes his case, starts for*
23   *the door, then stops.)* **Oh yes, you won't be allowed any**
24   **luggage, Lionel, so don't worry about your fuschia silk**
25   **pajamas.**
26   **LIONEL:**   **What do you mean? Who are you?**
27   **RHAL:**   **Oh, my apologies! I am Delegate Rhal from Planet**
28   **Zond.** *(Takes out a business card, and offers it to LIONEL.)*
29   **LIONEL:**   **From Zond? With a business card? Really, you're**
30   **hardly what I expected!** *(Laughs condescendingly.)* **After all,**
31   **you knocked on the door just as if you were . . . human,**
32   **and you look . . . well, you look human!**
33   **RHAL:**   **We try to appear in the guise most acceptable to our**
34   **candidates. It eliminates culture shock!**
35   **LIONEL:**   **Well, how thoughtful of you.**

1   RHAL: Our computer reports that you spend much time
2   looking at your image so I assumed a form somewhat
3   similar to your own. Not, of course, as perfect.
4   LIONEL: Oh, now you're teasing me!
5   RHAL: *(Turning to leave)* I shall see you at the launching. I
6   have one more candidate to interview. As a matter of
7   fact, I believe the computer has designated her as your
8   mate.
9   LIONEL: Mate? Really, how disgusting! If I wished a mate,
10   mumsy would interview her. But since I don't wish one,
11   you can save yourself some time!
12   RHAL: Lionel, surely you understood the nature of the
13   expedition when you submitted your application as a
14   candidate?
15   LIONEL: I was encouraged by a very highly placed official
16   to allow your planet the opportunity of enlisting me. I
17   did *not* "submit an application"!
18   RHAL: But you knew that our project was to assemble a
19   group of characteristic specimens of earthpeople to
20   populate our Earth microcosm on Zond?
21   LIONEL: That sounds like a laboratory experiment!
22   RHAL: But you were aware that we were selecting typical
23   specimens to . . .
24   LIONEL: Typical? Characteristic? What on earth are you
25   talking about? I am neither typical nor characteristic! I
26   am PERFECT!
27   RHAL: Oh, yes.
28   LIONEL: I am far above the average. I am exceptional.
29   RHAL: I see. *(He returns to the table, opens his case, takes out the*
30   *file, opens it, tears up the document within it.)* **I'm glad we**
31   **discovered this error in time.** *(LIONEL returns to the mirror,*
32   *pleased with having asserted his perfection, but a little worried*
33   *by RHAL's reaction. RHAL at the door.)* **And Lionel?**
34   LIONEL: *(Expectantly)* **Yes?**
35   RHAL: I'm very sorry about your mother.

1 LIONEL: *(Arrogantly)* **Oh, don't you worry about mumsy and**
2   **me. We'll make out just fine.** **And when you come back**
3   **looking for superior people, you can look me up again.**
4   **Perhaps then I'll consider your offer.**
5 RHAL: **Lionel ... I ... Lionel ... your   mother   is   out**
6   **there ... dead. The fog, you know.** *(LIONEL is transfixed.)*
7 LIONEL: *(Terrified)* **Mumsy?** *(RHAL takes the suitcase off the*
8   *chair, helps LIONEL to sit.)*
9 RHAL: **I didn't realize at first that you didn't know.**
10 LIONEL: **How could she do this to me? Why ... I can't even**
11   **find my fuschia silk pajamas!**
12 RHAL: *(Again at the door)* **Well, goodby, Lionel. We won't be**
13   **back again so I'll just wish you ... luck!**
14 LIONEL: **You won't be back?**
15 RHAL: **Well, not for a millenium or so. You see, we only make**
16   **a single expedition to gather representative creatures to**
17   **stock our culture farm. Then when their home planet is**
18   **capable of habitation again, we can re-colonize it from**
19   **original stock, and start the experiment all over again.**
20 LIONEL: **What do you mean, "capable of habitation again"?**
21 RHAL: **Why, when the planet can support life again! You**
22   **know, some doomed planets mess up their atmospheric**
23   **balance for millions of years. Then we simply have to**
24   **postpone the next experiment until conditions are right.**
25 LIONEL: **Are you trying to tell me that this planet is doomed?**
26 RHAL: **You didn't know? Oh, I am sorry. I just assumed you**
27   **were aware that the fog ... Well, I guess that comes as a**
28   **shock, eh? I am sorry. Well, goodby, Lionel.**
29 LIONEL: **Wait! Don't go!** *(Pulling RHAL back into the room.)*
30   **Listen, Rhal, I'm not really that exceptional! I mean,**
31   **mumsy thought I was, but she could have been wrong!**
32   **And maybe I'm really just sort of ... well ... exceptionally**
33   **typical. I'm sure I'm just the kind of individual specimen**
34   **that would really tone up the colony. Rhal, you just can't**
35   **afford to leave me behind!**

1   **RHAL: I am truly sorry, Lionel, but** . . .
2   **LIONEL:**   *(Crying)* **But you can't leave me on a doomed planet!**
3   *(He clings to RHAL.)*
4   **RHAL: Lionel, I'm sorry, but** . . . *(He gives a quick jab at*
5   *LIONEL's midriff and LIONEL sinks to the floor. RHAL exits*
6   *quickly. A moment later, he passes the window in the swirling*
7   *fog, his respirator covering his face.)*
8   **LIONEL:**   *(Crying)* **Come back!** *(He crawls to the door, opens it,*
9   *but is met by a wall of swirling fog. He slams the door, goes back*
10   *to the table for the fogmask, puts it on and rushes out.)* **You**
11   **can't leave me here!** *(The door slams. LIONEL gropes his way*
12   *past the window in the direction taken by RHAL.)* **I'm Perfect**
13   **Perley! You need me!**
14
15
16
17
18
19
20
21
22
23
24
25
26
27
28
29
30
31
32
33
34
35

Love Scene:
Dominic and Sadie

Cast:

One woman   *One man*

Production Notes

Young actors often feel that "character" analysis and motivation are unnecessary in comedy. They are, however, just as important as in serious drama.

This sketch presents a clash of egos, each character driving to fulfill his own needs. Dominic's self-image is obvious. He sees himself as a dapper, finely organized man of considerable wisdom and sophistication. Sadie is the earth-mother, seeking comfort, willing to let outer display and non-essentials go in favor of inner contentment. Each wishes the company of the other, but on his own terms.

In this clash of wills, Dominic loses because his stomach betrays him. Other women may be more comely, but none can cook like Sadie can. So she wins by blackmail.

Preparation: An interesting acting preparation takes the form of an improvisation that plays out the basic plot of the sketch but substitutes a raccoon for Dominic and a plowhorse for Sadie. Improvise lines to propel the plot forward but have Dominic-raccoon concentrate on the fastidious, almost coy mannerism of his species and have Sadie-horse concentrate on the complacent, ponderous and careful manner of her species. Then return to human form but try to maintain some of the spirit of the animal characters.

The acting style in this play is totally non-realistic. The play is almost like a musical comedy, with dance routines, numerous poses, and exaggerated acting.

Preparation: To get into the mood for this, try Workshop 15, *Taking Off* on developing plays in poetic form.

There is a definite Irish rhythm to the dialog here. Even if the pronunciation is not accurate, the actors' speech rhythm must be correct or the sketch simply will not work.

Love Scene:
Dominic and Sadie

Time: Mid-morning.

Scene: A back alley. The backdrop consists of the back entrances to three establishments; UR a mauve door discreetly labeled "MILADY'S BEAUTY EMPORIUM" beside which is one mauve plastic garbage can; just R of Center, a scarred green door marked "SADIE'S DINER" with three battered overflowing metal cans; and far UL a white door marked "CHEZ LORRAINE — FASHION GOWNS" with one white plastic can, and a couple of torn dress boxes spilling out tissue paper.

 DOMINIC enters from UL. He is middle-aged, cheerful, neither ugly nor handsome. He is dressed in a white spotlessly clean coverall with "DOMINIC'S DISPOSAL" between the shoulderblades. On his head at a jaunty angle is a baseball cap.

 He crosses the stage from L to R, doing an abbreviated soft-shoe routine (and perhaps whistling); glancing at the white can and the accompanying boxes he clucks in disapproval, passing the metal cans he grimaces and rolls his eyes heavenward, arriving at the mauve can, he stops, smiles, takes off his cap, and executes a gallant bow to the can. He puts on his cap again, takes white work gloves from his pocket, puts them on, flexes his fingers, picks up the mauve can, raises it very high, gazing at it with open-mouthed rapture. He holds this pose for a moment, and then responding to some inner music, he lowers it to shoulder height and still smiling, executes a ballroom waltz step and dances with it across the stage to exit stage L.

Sound Effect: *garbage dumping*

 In a moment, DOMINIC re-enters with the can, which he now tangos back to its original position. He puts it down, another gallant bow, and turns to the left to survey SADIE's garbage cans. The smile disappears, he removes his white gloves, pockets them, takes out soiled gray gloves, puts them on. He advances to the first can, head averted Downstage, a look of excruciating

1   *pain on his face, he picks it up. Holding it at arm's length, he*
2   *does a hesitation step funeral march across the stage, head*
3   *averted, nose raised, Offstage Left.*
4   Sound Effect: *garbage dumping*
5   *He returns as before, funeral march, replaces the can. He*
6   *turns to the next can; same procedure, but this time as if anxious*
7   *to get it over with, he does a knees-high gallop. On the ground*
8   *when he removes the can are two tin-cans and some cabbage*
9   *leaves. Exit Offstage Left.*
10   Sound Effect: *garbage dumping*
11   *He gallops back, replaces the can, and turns to the third*
12   *one. This is more than he can bear; the can is disintegrating,*
13   *one handle hangs loose, the shape of the lid bears no relationship*
14   *to the shape of the can. He moans in despair, averts his head*
15   *Downstage, reaches for the can, begins to pick it up. The handle*
16   *gives way, the can drops, spills out an assortment of tin-cans*
17   *and food packages. DOMINIC checks his coveralls: one pant leg*
18   *is besmirched. He wipes at it in disgust. A sigh of anguish*
19   *directed to the audience! Now affronted by this indignity, he*
20   *begins nudging the can across the stage with his feet, executing*
21   *a rather grim flamenco step. Exit Left.*
22   Sound Effect: *garbage dumping*
23   *After a moment the can arrives back alone propelled across*
24   *the stage as if by one almighty kick. It settles quivering DR.*
25   *DOMINIC re-enters, removing the soiled gloves. He stands L of*
26   *Center while he replaces these in his pocket, and takes out his*
27   *white ones. As he performs this business, the door URC opens*
28   *and SADIE stands framed in it.*
29   *SADIE is in her middle years, in a well-worn green*
30   *uniform, an almost white apron, and white comfort oxfords. She*
31   *is solid and unlovely, but she is not without a certain charm:*
32   *she can cook!*
33   *SADIE looks at the can DR, at the garbage spilled UC,*
34   *and then at DOMINIC. She cocks her head on one side, purses*
35   *her lips. She folds her arms.*

1   *DOMINIC glides over to the white garbage can, looks again*
2   *at the white gloves, is about to put them on when SADIE speaks.*
3   SADIE: Dominic, me dear.
4   DOMINIC: *(Turning graciously)* **Yeah, Sadie me angel?**
5   SADIE: Ya missed some a me garbage, me lovely.
6   DOMINIC: *(Sweetly)* **Ah Sadie, me love, I took all what was**
7   **put out decent-like.**
8   SADIE: *(Equally sweet)* **Dominic dear, I put all me garbage**
9   out decent.
10   DOMINIC: *(Losing his gallantry)* **The devil ya do. Ya left a pile**
11   **a slops on the ground!**
12   SADIE: *(Firing up)* **I did NOT! Ya spilled it when ya picked**
13   **up the can!**
14   DOMINIC: Pick up the can? It ain't possible ta pick up that
15   can. It ain't got any handles left. It's more decayin' than
16   yer garbage!
17   SADIE: There's nothin' wrong with me garbage cans nor me
18   garbage. It's as good as anyone else's.
19   DOMINIC: What? *(He goes to the can DR.)* It's fallin' apart, it
20   is! *(He kicks it.)*
21   SADIE: *(Coming down to L of DOMINIC.)* It's good for years yet
22   if ya don't kick it around. Ya garbage men are all alike!
23   Beat up me garbage cans and then complain cause they're
24   all beat up!
25   DOMINIC: Look, Sadie, I ain't destroyin' your perishin' can.
26   It's old age what's troublin' it. Old age!
27   SADIE: It ain't that old. It'll do for years yet. I'll not spend
28   me hard-earned cash on fancy purple cans to impress the
29   back alley trade like some others I could mention.
30   DOMINIC: Don't go sneerin' at Milady's now. She puts out
31   mighty pretty garbage, she does.
32   SADIE: Pretty garbage, is it?
33   DOMINIC: The state of yer garbage indicates the state of
34   yer mind, Sadie!
35   SADIE: Then if Milady's can is mostly empty?

1   DOMINIC: Ye've a wicked tongue, Sadie, a wicked sland'rous

2   tongue! Milady's garbage is neat and inoffensive-like and

3   indicates a mind that is sweet and troublin' to no one.

4   SADIE: *(Brushes past him, picks up the can and takes it UC beside*

5   *the other cans.)* Because there's no mind there at all ta

6   trouble, the daft, frizzle-stopped ninny!

7   DOMINIC: Ah Sadie, Sadie! Ya know yer at fault so yer laying

8   around at poor innocents!

9   SADIE: A purple can and the tart is innocent!

10   DOMINIC: Look now, Sadie, it's not just that it's purple; Chez

11   Lorraine's is white and . . .

12   SADIE: And her garbage is spillin' over!

13   DOMINIC: Just shows a mind a wee bit hasty! *(SADIE begins*

14   *to pick up the spilled garbage, throwing the tins into the can,*

15   *punctuating her speeches with the crash of metal on metal.)*

16   SADIE: Hasty? *(Crash!)* Her slops is muckin' the alley and

17   she's hasty. Mine does it and I'm indecent! *(Crash!)*

18   DOMINIC: Ah come now, Sadie, ye've got ta admit . . .

19   SADIE: Dominic, ye're a fool. *(Crash!)* A blind fool!

20   Completely blinded by pretty empty-headed garbage!

21   *(Crash!)*

22   DOMINIC: A fool, am I? *(Insulted, he moves to exit Stage Left.)*

23   SADIE: A blind fool! If I put me slops out bundled in tissue

24   and festooned in tinsel, ya'd think me mind was gorgeous!

25   *(Crash!)*

26   DOMINIC: *(Turning back to her)* Come now, Sadie, I wasn't

27   meanin' ta lay scorn on ya. But . . .

28   SADIE: No buts, Dominic, no buts! Ye've ruined forever our

29   relationship! *(She straightens up from her task.)*

30   DOMINIC: *(Coming to her)* Ah, Sadie girl . . .

31   SADIE: *(Sadly)* No more chats over warm blueberry tart with

32   sour cream sauce, no more lingerin' tête-a-têtes over ham

33   and egg pie, never another tryst amidst the steam of steak

34   and kidney pudd, alas, no blissful moments . . .

35   DOMINIC: Sadie, yer bein' too harsh, girl! I never said . . .

1   SADIE: . . . no more blissful moments sipping me own special
2   tea. *(Abruptly demanding)* **Never said what? Never said me**
3   **mind was indecent, did ya?**
4   DOMINIC: **Now, Sadie, yer filling me mouth with words!**
5   SADIE: **And that's all I'll ever fill it with again, ya back alley**
6   **Casanova!**
7   DOMINIC: *(Anguished)* **Sadie, dear girl, ya don't know what**
8   **yer sayin'!** *(SADIE folds her arms, standing guard beside the*
9   *remaining garbage.)*
10   SADIE: **Don't ya Sadie girl me!** *(Rapidly DOMINIC begins to*
11   *pick up the remaining garbage. SADIE does not move, staring*
12   *straight ahead. He has to get down on hands and knees to get*
13   *the last of it from behind the garbage cans. He rises, his task*
14   *complete.)* **I'll be goin' in now. Me turnovers will be ready**
15   **to come outa me oven.**
16   DOMINIC: **Turnovers? Your rhubarb cream turnovers?**
17   SADIE: **The same.** *(She goes to the door.)*
18   DOMINIC: **Sadie, if ye'll wait just a moment, I'll hold the**
19   **door for ya.** *(Quickly, he puts on his white gloves, advances to*
20   *the door, but she bars his way; she is looking significantly at the*
21   *offending garbage can. DOMINIC understands. He advances on*
22   *the can smartly, for a brief moment he contemplates removing*
23   *his white gloves, realizes it would be a tactical error, picks up*
24   *the can, embraces it closely and does a speedy minuet Offstage*
25   *Left with it.)*
26   *Sound Effect: garbage dumping*
27   *SADIE's eyes glitter triumphantly. He returns minuetting*
28   *briskly, deposits the can with great care. SADIE turns again to*
29   *the door, he bustles over, opens it. She exits. He pauses briefly*
30   *to examine his soiled clothing with anguish, then with a final*
31   *"oh-what-the-heck" soft-shoe routine, he follows her Offstage.*
32
33
34
35

Fortunes

Cast:

One woman   Two men

Production Notes

This sketch can be seen as an exercise in pacing dialog. There are long pauses as the old lady controls her emotions, as the son gropes for words to move her to compassion. Elsewhere, the dialog speeds in rapid-fire questions and answers. Decide, before the actors begin learning lines, how the sketch will be paced so that pacing and words will fit easily together.

Preparation: Draw a plot graph in pencil in the margin of the script with wavy lines where the pace is rapid and dotted lines where there are pauses and slow reactions, as a reminder to the actors both during rehearsals and during memorization.

Like *In the Middle of the Night,* this sketch requires very little physical action. The old man enters, sits, gets up and leaves. The old woman moves back and forth from fireplace to table, but never becomes physically involved with the old man, and only briefly rests her hand on her son. The son moves between the two old people.

The temptation for young actors is to complicate the action to add "interest". This is neither necessary nor desirable. They must learn that all stage action must be purposeful. If there is no reason to move or to gesture, they must not do so. Furthermore, in plays of this type, increased physical action takes the focus off the dialog where the tension and therefore audience interest should remain.

Fortunes is also an exercise in listening. The actors must realize when their characters are "turned off" to the other's words, when they are only pretending to be turned off, and when they openly comprehend the words spoken to them. These variations in attention are due to the subtext of the play, the things that the characters are really driving towards. For the old woman, acceptance of the stranger as her long absent husband would also mean acceptance of her own unloveliness. Hers is a negative drive: "I will not acknowledge this man," and she hears only that which will not derail her drive. But her son keeps undermining her efforts with new facts that she finds increasingly difficult to ignore. He is playing a very subtle sort of game, maneuvering the old lady into a trap. What has he to gain by this? Is he aware of his motives? What is his drive in the play? How about the old man's character?

Preparation: Students might try one of the variations in Workshop 5, *The Prisoner, Tunnels,* or *The Factory* — for the feeling of physical entrapment that each of these characters must feel.

YOUR NOTES

Fortunes

Time: During the last century.

Scene: A village in Central Europe. The common room of a peasant house. A hearth fire URC, a door DL, a table and two chairs DR, a high-back settee UL.

Characters: An old woman (MOTHER) is stirring a pot of stew suspended over the fire. Her clothing is homespun, she is quite unattractive in appearance, but it is obvious from her first words that she is a dominant personality.

The door opens and two men enter. The first is the SON, approaching middle-age, in homespun, dressed for outdoors, carrying a traveling satchel. The second is the OLD MAN, wizened, bearded, bewildered, and apparently senile. His clothes are different in style from the son's, but are worn and drab. He carries a bundle under his arm.

At Rise: The woman starts, turns to them, dropping the stirring spoon. She comes toward them, her face hardening. She stops Center Stage, face now impassive; she turns to face DR.

SON: *(Hopefully)* **Mother, I've brought him home.**

MOTHER: *(After a pause, flatly)* **He isn't the right one.**

SON: *(Puzzled)* **He said his name is Peter.**

MOTHER: **He's NOT the right one.**

SON: **His name is Peter.** *(Pause while he leads the OLD MAN to the settee.)* **He didn't want to come.**

MOTHER: **Of course.** *(Returns to her work at the hearth.)*

SON: *(Seating the OLD MAN, who puts his bundle beside him on the settee.)* **He had lived in that place a long time. They said . . .**

MOTHER: **Who?**

SON: **The people there, his neighbors.**

MOTHER: **Oh.**

SON: **They said he had been there a long time, before they had come there.** *(Pause)* **Any of them.**

1   **MOTHER: His name is Peter?**
2   **SON: Yes.** *(Moves to the table DR.)*
3   **MOTHER: He said that himself?**
4   **SON: Yes, he said his name is Peter. No other name. Only**
5   **Peter.** *(Pause, as she looks across at the OLD MAN, who is*
6   *motionless, apparently unaware of the conversation.)* **They**
7   **said ... his neighbors ... that he had no other name when**
8   **they came there. Just Peter.**
9   **MOTHER:** *(Coming to the table with plates from the hearthside.)*
10   **He had been there a long time?**
11   **SON: Years.**
12   **MOTHER:** *(Bitingly)* **And his name is just ... Peter.**
13   **SON:** *(Patiently)* **Yes, just Peter ... He lived there alone for**
14   **years.** *(Pause)* **With his dog.**
15   **MOTHER:** *(Turns to look at the OLD MAN.)* **He had a dog?**
16   **SON: Yes. A mongrel.**
17   **MOTHER: Oh.**
18   **SON: It died.**
19   **MOTHER:** *(After a pause)* **Yes?**
20   **SON: The dog. It died. So he lived alone then.**
21   **MOTHER: For years, you said.** *(She looks away from the OLD*
22   *MAN, back to her son.)*
23   **SON:** *(Nods)* **He farmed his land there ... in the old fashion.**
24   **He fished.**
25   **MOTHER:** *(Turns her back on her son and returns to the hearth.)*
26   **What will you do with him?**
27   **SON: Do with him?**
28   **MOTHER:** *(Over her shoulder)* **Yes. You've brought him a long**
29   **way. What will you do with him now?**
30   **SON:** *(Patiently)* **Care for him here.**
31   **MOTHER:** *(Turning to her SON)* **He's not the right one.**
32   **SON:** *(Going to stand beside the settee between his MOTHER and*
33   *the OLD MAN.)* **Mother, his name is Peter, he ...**
34   **MOTHER:** *(Raising her voice)* **He's not Peter Elaiyeff!** *(The OLD*
35   *MAN turns his head slowly; he appears to be listening.)*

1   SON: ... he farmed his land there in our fashion. *(Pause)*
2   He ...
3   MOTHER: Does he have our language?
4   SON: He fished just as we fish. He ...
5   MOTHER: Does he have our language? *(Pause. She returns to*
6   *the fireplace.)*
7   SON: No .... he has forgotten it. So many years he lived in
8   their land.
9   MOTHER: No.
10   SON: And then he lived alone. Only the dog to ...
11   MOTHER: No! He is not Peter Elaiyeff! *(The OLD MAN turns*
12   *his head again, this time anxiously, somehow challenged by her*
13   *voice.)*
14   SON: But we must take care of him, now that they sent for
15   us to fetch him ... home.
16   MOTHER: *(Carrying the pot of stew to the table)* Did they say
17   how they knew to send to us?
18   SON: He had old letters and documents. When they found
19   he had grown simple, they ...
20   MOTHER: What letters were they?
21   SON: *(Coming to her at the table)* Old ones. Old ones written to
22   Peter Elaiyeff.
23   MOTHER: What letters?
24   SON: From our village. *(Gently)* From you.
25   MOTHER: *(Angrily)* He does not have our lauguage. How
26   could he read letters from me?
27   SON: He has only forgotten the language.
28   MOTHER: I wrote letters to Peter Elaiyeff, not to that man!
29   *(Points past her son at the OLD MAN.)* That man without our
30   language!
31   SON: He had letters written to Peter Elaiyeff in our
32   language ... He kept them in a sea chest.
33   MOTHER: *(Staring past her son at the OLD MAN.)* He had a sea
34   chest?
35   SON: Yes. A sea chest with his initials carved on it. A

1   **blackened oak chest.** *(The MOTHER is still staring at the*
2   *OLD MAN; he stares back as if trying to recognize her.)*
3   MOTHER: *(Speaking quietly)* **When I sent Peter Elaiyeff to**
4   **make his fortune, he had a dark oak sea chest on his**
5   **shoulder. He carved his initials on it in the days before**
6   **he went away.**
7   SON: *(Gently)* **On its lid. The initials were carved on its lid.**
8   MOTHER: *(With growing bitterness)* **He walked out that door,**
9   **the black chest on his shoulder, his mongrel hound at**
10   **his heels. I told him to send for me when he'd made his**
11   **fortune. To send for me and my child.** *(Still staring at the*
12   *OLD MAN, she pats her son's arm. At last recognition comes*
13   *into the face of the OLD MAN; he looks around, recognizing the*
14   *room.)*
15   SON: **Yes, mother, I know.**
16   MOTHER: *(Viciously)* **But he didn't make his fortune!** *(The*
17   *OLD MAN begins to smile; it is a smile of pure defiance.)* **For**
18   **he never came back ... He never sent for me ... He died**
19   **there. He died in that country many, many years ago.**
20   *(The OLD MAN's smile softens to pity and he slowly shakes his*
21   *head at her. He bends, picks up his bundle and moves towards*
22   *the door. MOTHER almost pleading.)* **If he had lived he would**
23   **have come back for me ...** *(The OLD MAN quietly exits*
24   *wihout looking back again.)*
25   SON: **Mother, look at him again ...** *(Turns)* **He's gone!** *(He runs*
26   *out after him.)*
27   MOTHER: **No, come back!** *(Pause. She sits down, alone now.)* **He**
28   **would have sent for me ...**
29
30
31
32
33
34
35

Walking Back

Cast:

One man   One woman

Production Notes

Each of the actors in this sketch has a different acting problem, to be dealt with in specific ways.

The Soldier: The actor must deal with three separate relationships — man, and mother, man and wife (or lover), man and daughter. What emotions does each of these persons arouse in him? What is the reason that he sees them at this particular time in the middle of a war, when he is, perhaps, in the act of desertion?

He establishes an attitude to each one but modifies it as he becomes involved in the relationship, so that within the play, he acts out three different growing involvements. However, each succeeding relationship is tempered by the outcome of the preceding one. Each is influenced by an increasing feeling of frustration and loss, and less willingness to accept the reality of the event. Finally he realizes that even the child is gone, but at the same time he recognizes that the panic and hysteria he felt at his arrival in this place are also gone. The actor must present this growth in the young man's character subtly. It is somehow a more mature young man who is left to make his decision at the end of the play. I do not believe, incidentally, that he returns to battle, but the actors must decide this question for themselves.

The Woman: She must invent three fresh and distinct characterizations. She must not spill the mannerisms of one onto the next. For example, each handles a stick (in the case of the old woman, a substitute for the stick) and each uses it in a different way. But the actor must regard the stick each time from her new status. Her very hands must be those of a new character. Similarly, the carriage of head and shoulders, voice rhythm and tone must alter. Finally she must regard the young man from three different vantage points. What does a mother expect in the relationship with her son, a wife (or lover) in the relationship with her man, a girl-child with her father? Furthermore, what does each one *demand* of him?

The actor must spend as much time as is necessary *observing* for this role. She must closely examine her own and other family situations, and she must observe and mentally catalog mannerisms and gestures that will make each character distinctive.

Preparation: To prepare actors for changing roles and fresh characterizations, try *Rotating Encounters* or *Take-Off* (Workshop 22 and 23).

This sketch is one of the few in this book which is definitely improved with special effects. The lighting suggested is not difficult to achieve but makes a decided difference in establishing mood.

Preparation: To examine the possibilities in lighting sets for mood, try *Table-Top Sets* (Workshop 19).

YOUR NOTES

1
2

Walking Back

3 **Scene:** An open area. Slightly L of C is an old packing crate about
4 three feet by four feet with stencils reading "CAUTION" and
5 "DANGER: EXPLOSIVES". Huddled against the Downstage
6 side of it is the woman, although at first she resembles only a
7 large pile of old rags. The light in this sketch is dim, most of it
8 centered on an area DR where a dilapidated street signpost
9 stands, its four directional markers almost illegible. Later
10 another area of light around the box will be used.
11   The sounds of a distant battle may be used throughout
12 the encounter; if used they should become more threatening
13 towards the end of the play.
14 **Characters:** THE WOMAN: she wears a peasant blouse which can
15 be pulled low to reveal shoulders and bosom, and a dark colored
16 flared skirt which reaches several inches below her knees, its
17 hem ragged and uneven. Over her blouse she clutches a huge
18 three-cornered shawl, once woven in gay colors, but now faded
19 and torn. On her head is an old hat, with ties that go under her
20 chin. It is pulled low covering every vestige of hair and ears,
21 and in fact nearly resting on her eyebrows. Her feet are bare,
22 and like everything else about her, they are filthy.
23   THE SOLDIER: a very young man, wearing a helmet and
24 carrying a rifle. He is in worn and dirty battledress, his left
25 sleeve ripped, revealing bloodied, makeshift bandages. His voice
26 is low and tense; he is fearful of every sound.
27 **At Rise:** Only the WOMAN is on stage, and she is so still that she
28 appears to be only a prop. The SOLDIER enters from UL and
29 runs to C. His breath is coming hard, and he is obviously terrified
30 and exhausted. He stops, looks back. Another step forward and
31 his glance fastens on the pile of rags. Alarmed, he raises his
32 rifle and backs away a step. Finally satisfied that it is no threat,
33 he lowers the gun, moves DR. He stops at the signpost to peer
34 up at the markers.
35 **SOLDIER:** *(Almost crying)* **I can't even read them!** *(He leans*

1 *against the post, takes off his helmet.)* **They couldn't show me**
2 **the way home, anyhow!** *(He begins to cry, then in an effort to*
3 *control himself, he sits down with his back against the post,*
4 *facing Stage L, and rubs at his eyes and nose with his sleeve.*
5 *Then, as he stares unseeingly at the pile of rags, the light begins*
6 *to increase in the area of the box and the rags begin to stir*
7 *revealing that it is the WOMAN. She sits up. The SOLDIER gets*
8 *slowly to his feet, beginning to back off DR, his rifle at the ready.)*
9 **WOMAN:** *(Reaching out to him, whining)* **Don't go!**
10 **SOLDIER:** **Stay there!**
11 **WOMAN:** **Don't be scared, boy, it's only me!**
12 **SOLDIER:** **Who are you?** *(WOMAN cackles.)* **Are you the**
13 **enemy?**
14 **WOMAN:** *(Cackling)* **Me? The enemy? It's all right. I won't**
15 **hurt you!**
16 **SOLDIER:** *(Backing off in order to keep her in sight.)* **Just stay**
17 **where you are!**
18 **WOMAN:** **Wait! You're not going to leave me here, are you?**
19 *(The SOLDIER stops, confused. WOMAN crying.)* **You weren't**
20 **going to, were you? You ... you'd just forgotten where**
21 **you left me, hadn't you?** *(The SOLDIER is more puzzled,*
22 *comes back a few steps, rests his rifle butt on the ground.)*
23 **SOLDIER:** **Listen, lady, I think ...**
24 **WOMAN:** *(Struggling to rise, very slowly inching herself up by*
25 *clinging to the box.)* **You didn't forget, did you, dearie?**
26 **SOLDIER:** **Do I know you?**
27 **WOMAN:** **Come, give me a hand.** *(He doesn't move.)* **I don't walk**
28 **so well now, dear. Not enough to eat, you know. They**
29 **keep all the food for the army. Said I was useless and I**
30 **might as well die! They don't care when you're old, you**
31 **know.** *(Even when standing, she is still a bent figure.)*
32 **SOLDIER:** **Who are you?**
33 **WOMAN:** *(Cackling)* **But you came back for me, didn't you?**
34 **SOLDIER:** **No! I don't know you.**
35 **WOMAN:** *(Tottering toward him)* **We'll go along together now,**

1   **boy. We'll just go . . .** *(She falls in a grotesque heap.)*

2   **SOLDIER: Look, you can't stay there!** *(She starts to moan,*

3   *rocking back and forth.)* **Those tanks will be coming back**

4   **along this road! You'll be safer where you were.** *(She*

5   *continues to rock and moan.)* **Come on, grannie, up you get!**

6   *(He approaches her. Almost as if she had only been bluffing in*

7   *order to force him to approach, the WOMAN grasps his rifle,*

8   *and begins to pull herself up using it as her support.)*

9   **WOMAN: Not as old as that, dearie! I've not that many years!**

10   **It's only the bad times and the cold that's put the lines**

11   **in my . . .**

12   **SOLDIER:** *(Laughing at her conceit, and beginning to help her up.)*

13   **All right then, little mother, up on your feet!**

14   **WOMAN:** *(Upright now, clutching the rifle, cackling triumphantly)*

15   **There now! You did remember me! My son, my little boy!**

16   *(She reaches a hand to his face but nearly topples over again.)*

17   **SOLDIER:** *(Steadying her)* **Look, I'm not your son! You're**

18   **confused. Little mother is just . . . just a term for an . . . for**

19   **a woman, you know!**

20   **WOMAN:** *(Cackling)* **Well, you'd hardly call some man your**

21   **mother, would you, son? Come now, we'll go. I'll use this**

22   **for my walking stick.** *(She clutches his gun.)*

23   **SOLDIER: No, you can't have that!**

24   **WOMAN: But I must have a stick. This will do fine, just fine,**

25   **you'll see. I just knew my boy would come back for me!**

26   **SOLDIER: No, look now. I'll get you a real stick to walk with.**

27   **Come, you wait over there.** *(He begins to lead her back to the box.)*

28   **WOMAN:** *(Clinging to him, shrieking)* **You're trying to leave me**

29   **again!**

30   **SOLDIER: Sh-h-h-h, little mother. They'll hear us! Just trust**

31   **me now. I'll find a walking stick.** *(He puts her down beside*

32   *the box.)*

33   **WOMAN: You won't leave me?** *(She crawls after him as he starts*

34   *to go.)*

35   **SOLDIER:** *(Patiently, having now accepted her as his*

1   *responsibility.)* **No, no, mother, I'm not going to forget you**

2   **again.** *(He puts her back beside the box again.)* **You wait here**

3   **in case the tanks come back while I'm gone. I'll find you**

4   **a stout walking stick, and then we'll see if we can't find**

5   **some food and maybe a roof, eh?**

6   **WOMAN:**   **You'll come back for me? You won't forget, my son?**

7   **SOLDIER:** *(Moving DR)* **I won't forget, mother. I'll look after**

8   **you. Just wait here, and I won't be long.** *(Exit DR. As soon*

9   *as he leaves, she begins fumbling with the shawl, unfastening*

10   *pins which hold it in place. Then she begins to stand again,*

11   *slowly clawing her way up the side of the box. But as she rises,*

12   *the shawl slides off her shoulders, and like an emerging butterfly,*

13   *she has gained a new form and a new strength. She is now a*

14   *young woman and quite beautiful. She pulls off her hat, allowing*

15   *it to hang on her back by its ties, and shakes her hair loose. It*

16   *is long and unkempt, and she runs her fingers through it to tidy*

17   *it. Now she is ready for the SOLDIER's return, and she leans*

18   *against the box to wait for him.)*

19   **SOLDIER:** *(Returning DR, a stick about a yard long in his hand.*

20   *He begins to call softly before he is in view.)* **Here it is, mother!**

21   **And there's an old house down the road . . .** *(He stops R of*

22   *C, looks at the WOMAN, then confused, looks behind the box,*

23   *ending DL. The WOMAN watches expressionlessly.)* **Where did**

24   **she go? I told her to stay right here!**

25   **WOMAN:** *(Gently)* **She's gone.**

26   **SOLDIER:** **I can see that! She can't be far . . . She . . . she can't**

27   **even walk!** *(He crosses DR again, peering into the gloom, calling*

28   *softly.)* **Mother!**

29   **WOMAN:** **She's gone. Anyhow you don't need her.**

30   **SOLDIER:** **But she needs me.** *(Calling)* **Mother!**

31   **WOMAN:** **I told you she's gone.**

32   **SOLDIER:** **Mother!**

33   **WOMAN:** **Hey! What about me?**

34   **SOLDIER:** *(Turning to look her over.)* **You? You can take care**

35   **of yourself!** *(The WOMAN shrugs and turns away.)* **Well, you**

1   can, can't you? I mean, that's what you've been doing in
2   this war, isn't it? *(He starts to move away DR. She turns to*
3   *watch him and then finally speaks.)*
4   WOMAN: What about you? *(The SOLDIER stops.)* Can you take
5   care of yourself?
6   SOLDIER: *(Facing her)* Sure I can! That's a dumb thing to ask
7   a soldier!
8   WOMAN: You weren't always a soldier.
9   SOLDIER: And that's a dumb thing to say, too.
10   WOMAN: You were a lot more than that once.
11   SOLDIER: Oh, sure, I was a real dealer before the war!
12   WOMAN: *(Smiling)* A dealer in summer picnics and winter
13   ski runs, and you used to . . .
14   SOLDIER: Skis? I don't ski!
15   WOMAN: You used to wear soft sweaters, and you carried a
16   banner in peace rallies, and you rode a bike with the
17   gang in the park, and read the *Iliad,* and watched the
18   Saturday night hockey games, and danced . . .
19   SOLDIER: Are you crazy? That's wasn't me! I never did . . .
20   WOMAN: And you loved me.
21   SOLDIER: I don't even know you! *(He comes toward her.)*
22   WOMAN: And on summer nights we went skinny-dipping in
23   the river, and listened to old Beatle records, and . . .
24   SOLDIER: I don't know you! *(She smiles.)* It wasn't me! I don't
25   know you!
26   WOMAN: *(Softly)* And you loved me.
27   SOLDIER: No.
28   WOMAN: You held me close in the dark. *(She steps closer.)*
29   SOLDIER: It wasn't me.
30   WOMAN: And you kissed me. *(She kisses him gently on the*
31   *mouth.)*
32   SOLDIER: Look, I'm sure I'd have remembered you. But it
33   just wasn't . . . *(She kisses him again. He drops the stick and*
34   *the gun.)* Was it me? Did I do all those things?
35   WOMAN: Remember how we danced? *(She moves into his arms*

1   *and begins to sway to an unheard melody. For a moment he*
2   *stands stiffly, then slowly relaxes and begins to sway with her.)*
3   **SOLDIER:**   It seems so long ago, almost like it never
4   **happened.** *(They dance quietly for a few moments. Then*
5   *abruptly he stops and steps away from her.)* **This is stupid!**
6   **Right here in the middle of the road! The tanks could**
7   **come this way any minute!** *(He runs UC peering into the*
8   *gloom.)*
9   **WOMAN:**   *(Bending down to pick up the stick)* **We used to talk a**
10   **lot about what we were going to do . . . about our future.**
11   **SOLDIER:**   *(Coming back to her)* **Yeah?**
12   **WOMAN:**   You were going to become very rich and
13   **famous . . . and I wanted a home . . . and maybe children.**
14   *(She draws patterns on the ground with the stick.)*
15   **SOLDIER:**   A home . . . with me?
16   **WOMAN:**   I think so. *(She smiles and begins to draw a house on*
17   *the ground.)* **Just a little house with a funny chimney like**
18   **this.** *(She draws and he laughs at the comic chimney.)* **And**
19   **curtains in the windows, and gardens full of daffodils**
20   **and lilacs.**
21   **SOLDIER:**   *(Pointing at her drawing and laughing)* **What's that?**
22   **WOMAN:**   *(Laughing)* **The daffodils, of course!**
23   **SOLDIER:**   Hey, just a minute! There's a house like that down
24   **the road! I was just there!** *(He starts off L; and stops.)* **No,**
25   **it was down THAT road!** *(He returns as far as the signpost.)*
26   **No, it was . . . I've forgotten!** *(He stands looking at the signpost*
27   *and while he continues to talk she makes the transition which*
28   *follows: She returns to the box and sits on the ground, her back*
29   *against the box, drawing up her knees. She pulls up her skirt to*
30   *expose one knee in order to scratch it and pick at a scab formed*
31   *there. Next she pushes her hair behind her ears, and replaces*
32   *the hat straight on her head in the manner of a small child. She*
33   *draws the neck of her blouse up as high as possible. Finally she*
34   *puts her thumb in her mouth, picks up the stick and begins to*
35   *beat it rhythmically on the ground, humming monotonously as*

she does so. Even after the SOLDIER turns to her, she continues beating and humming, although more quietly.) **I was standing right here and then . . . then she came along . . . my mother . . . and I went to get her a walking stick . . . and that's when I saw the house. And there were daffodils around it . . . but when I came back, she was gone . . . I told her to wait here . . . She promised me she would . . . She said . . .** *(He turns to the WOMAN who has completed the transition.)* **Darling?** *(He goes closer.)* **But you're not her!** *(He peers into the gloom UL; returns to stand just L of the WOMAN.)* **She's gone, too, hasn't she? I thought she really needed me.** *(He looks as if he will cry again.)* **She said she did. She said she loved me and we'd live in a funny little house and . . . She needed me, I know she did!** *(Angrily to the woman)* **Stop that damned racket!** *(The WOMAN starts to whimper, the thumb still in her mouth. She drops the stick, grabs the shawl, cradling it against her cheek and stroking it. He bends down to her.)* **Oh, now look, I'm sorry, but that noise was getting me. I didn't mean to scare you. What are you doing here anyway?** *(The WOMAN snuffles and rocks back and forth, sucking her thumb and stroking her shawl.)* **C'mon, let's get out of here.** *(He puts a hand on her shoulder; she shakes him off and cringes away from him.)* **I'm not going to hurt you! Let's be friends, eh? Come on. You come with me and I'll find a safe place for us. OK?** *(She shakes her head, and tears start to roll down her face.)* **But honey, you can't stay here! Look, we'll go down that road and maybe we'll find some food for you and . . . we'll look for something warm for your feet.** *(He walks to R of C, and looks back at her.)* **Coming?** *(She begins to cry, her whole body shaking with sobs.)* **Well, for chrisake, kid, you can't stay here! We gotta get out of here!** *(She ignores him.)* **Look, what do you want? I'm trying to help you, but I can't if I don't know what you want!** *(He returns to stand beside her.)* **Come on, kid, what is it?**

1   **WOMAN:**   *(Suddenly clasping his leg with both arms and sobbing*
2   *desperately.)* **Daddy! I want my daddy!**
3   **SOLDIER:**   *(Trying to pry her loose.)* **Oh no, you don't! I'm not**
4   **your daddy! You're not going to get me that way!**
5   **WOMAN:**   **Daddy! Daddy!**
6   **SOLDIER:**   *(Realizing that she is not going to give up.)* **All right,**
7   **kid, all right. I'll be your daddy. But let's get out of here!**
8   *(He turns to the R as she releases him. He walks to the signpost,*
9   *picks up his helmet, and turns to see if she is coming. But the*
10   *light in the area of the box is gone now and the place where the*
11   *WOMAN sat is only marked by a heap of rags. At last he puts*
12   *on his helmet, and picks up his rifle. He is ready to depart. As*
13   *the light dims out he stands looking at the signpost in an effort*
14   *to decide the road he should take.)*
15
16
17
18
19
20
21
22
23
24
25
26
27
28
29
30
31
32
33
34
35

APPENDIX: SUGGESTIONS FOR MUSIC

The music listed here includes classical, electronic, and jazz works, plus quite a number of selections that are not easily categorized.

Some of the titles certainly don't suggest the music within. However, the children will not be told the titles, so it matters not at all that Copland's Western drama *Billy the Kid* places them in a dungeon cell in "The Prisoner", or that sculpture is inspired by Holst's *The Planets*. It is only important that music be chosen which can evoke the necessary responses.

This appendix is divided into three sections. The first lists musical selections suggested for specific workshops. Each of these is keyed by number to the recordings listed in Sections Two and Three. Section Two is a "basic list" of recordings designed to make up a beginner's library of music for use in Creative Drama. (An asterisk in Section One identifies the basic recordings.) In many cases, one recording will contain several pertinent selections and will be useful in several different workshops. Section Three is an "extended list" — useful recordings which may be added to the basic list at a later date.

All recordings listed were available from their manufacturer when this handbook went to press. However, records are subject to periodic withdrawal by distributors so that some may be unavailable through local outlets.

There may be companies in other large cities, so it's worth investigating your telephone directory.

SUGGESTIONS FOR SPECIFIC WORKSHOPS

WORKSHOP NO. 1

Phase 1: Painting Boxes

*1 Debussy: La Mer
*2 Holst: The Planets (quieter movements)
*3 Dvorak: Serenade for Strings
18 Rodrigo: Concierto de Aranjuez (second movement)

Phase 2: Decorating Boxes

19 Prokofiev: The Stone Flower
*3 Dvorak: Serenade for Strings (faster sections)
*2 Holst: The Planets (Mercury and Uranus)
18 Rodrigo: Concierto de Aranjuez
*4 Tchaikovsky: Symphony No. 6 (second movement)

Phase 3: Decorating Small Objects

*5 Scarlatti: Sonatas for harpsichord
20 J. S. Bach: Goldberg Variations (harpsichord)
Debussy: Preludes and etudes for piano
Baroque music for lute or guitar

Phase 4: Group Painting

*6 Stravinsky: L'Histoire du Soldat
*4 Tchaikovsky: Symphony No. 6
21 Spike Jones: any available
*7 Pfeiffer: Electronomusic

WORKSHOP NO. 2 — HANDPLAYS

*8 Debussy: Jimbo's Lullaby in Children's Corner Suite
*8 Debussy: Five Preludes
*9 Copland: Rodeo
*10 Gould: Derivations for Clarinet and Band
22 Carlos: electronic music
*10 Copland: Concerto for Clarinet and Orchestra

WORKSHOP NO. 3 — SCULPTURE

23 Prokofiev: Romeo and Juliet
*2 Holst: The Planets (Uranus)
*4 Tchaikovsky: Symphony No. 6 (first movement)

WORKSHOP NO. 5 — THE PRISONER

24 Subotnick: *Sidewinder*
*9 Copland: *Billy the Kid*
*2 Holst: *The Planets* (Saturn)
*11 Schoenberg: *Five Pieces for Orchestra*

Variation No. 1 — Tunnels
*11 Schoenberg: *Five Pieces*
*2 Holst: *The Planets* (Mercury)

Variation No. 2 — The Factory
*12 Varese: *Ameriques*
*10 Stravinsky: *Ebony Concerto* (last movement)
*7 Pfeiffer: *Electronomusic* (After Hours)

WORKSHOP NO. 6 — MIRRORS AND SHADOWS

*3 Dvorak: *Serenade for Strings*
25 Tomita: "Snowflakes are Dancing"
*1 Debussy: Orchestral works
*13 Ravel: *Pavane*

WORKSHOP NO. 7 — MACHINES

26 Anderson: *Syncopated Clock*
*10 Bernstein: *Prelude, Fugue and Riffs*
*14 Partch: *Daphne of the Dunes and Castor and Pollux*
*6 Stravinsky: *L'Histoire du Soldat* (for more complete machines)
*10 Stravinsky: *Ebony Concerto* (first movement)
*10 Gould: *Variations* (third movement)

WORKSHOP NO. 8 — COMBAT

*10 Copland: *Concerto for Clarinet and Orchestra* (first portion)
*10 Gould: *Derivations* (second movement)
27 Respighi: *The Fountains of Rome* (first section)
Also the music suggested for Mirrors and Shadows, Workshop No. 6

WORKSHOP NOS. 16 THROUGH 19

Select music from suggestions for Workshop No. 20

WORKSHOP NO. 20 — DISASTERS

*15 Subotnick; *Silver Apples of the Moon*
28 Stravinsky: *The Rite of Spring* (will require an added portion of quiet "wind-down" music — a portion of Tchaikovsky's final movement of *Symphony No. 6* would do very well)

40 Pink Floyd: *A Saucerful of Secrets*

Variation No. 1 — Primitive Man
*14 Partch: *The World of Harry Partch*
*16 Takemitsu: *Water Music*
 *6 Milhaud: *Creation of the World*
*12 Milhaud: *L'Homme et Son Desir*
 29 Miles Davis: *Bitches' Brew*

Variation No. 2 — Story music
Traveling Music
*10 Gould: *Derivations* (last movement)
 *7 Pfeiffer: *Electronomusic* (Take-off)
 30 Prokofiev: *Alexander Nevsky* (Battle on the Ice)
*17 Mussorgsky: *Pictures at an Exhibition* (Promenade; The Old Castle)
 31 Verdi: *Aida* (March)
*12 Honegger: *Pacific 231* (to suggest trains)
*13 Ibert: *Escales*
 *7 Pfeiffer: *Electronomusic* (Reflections on a String — to suggest
      flying carpets)
Chases:
 32 Rossini: *William Tell Overture*
 *1 Ravel: *Daphnis & Chloe*
 *2 Holst: *The Planets* (Mercury)
*17 Mussorgsky: *Pictures at an Exhibition* (The Hut of Baba Yaga;
      Ballet of the Chicks in their Shells)
Places:
*13 Chabrier: *Espana*
*13 Ibert: *Escales*
 22 Mimaroglu: *Le tombeau d'Edgar Poe*
 27 Respighi: *The Fountains of Rome; The Pines of Rome*
*17 Mussorgsky: *Pictures at an Exhibition*
 29 Miles Davis: *Bitches' Brew*
Moods:
 33 Mystic Moods Orchestra: any one of their recordings
 29 Miles Davis: *In a Silent Way; Kind of Blue*
 34 Environments Disc I (for waves and seasounds) *The Psychologi-
      cally Ultimate Seashore;* (for songbirds) *Optimum Aviary*
 35 Environments Disc II (for bells) *Tintinnabulation*
 36 Dvorak: *Symphony No. 9* (opening movement)
*17 Mussorgsky: *Pictures at an Exhibition* (Gnomes; The Market
      Place at Limoges)
 37 Paul Horn: *Inside II* (for storms, forest fires, seashore, traveling
      through space — *The Mahabhutas Elements)*
Celebrations and Ceremonies:
 *8 Debussy: *Golliwog's Cake Walk*
 25 Tomita: "Snowflakes are Dancing"
 38 Berlioz: *Roman Carnival*
 *4 Tchaikovsky: *Symphony No. 6* (third movement)
 39 Calliope music for circus and carnival effects

Sound Trips:
*7 Pfeiffer: *Electronomusic*
22 Lewin-Richter: *Study No. 1*
22 Mimaroglu: *Bowery Bum*

WORKSHOP NO. 21

Old Folks Home:
*4 Tchaikovsky: *Symphony No. 6* (final movement)
36 Dvorak: *Symphony No. 9* (second movement)
*2 Holst: *The Planets* (Saturn)

Variation No. 3 — The New Settlement and
Variation No. 4 — The Fortress
36 Dvorak: *Symphony No. 9*

Variation No. 5 — The Sailing Ship
34 Environment Disc No. 1: *The Psychologically Ultimate Seashore*
37 Paul Horn: *Inside II (The Mahabhutas* — water)
36 Dvorak: *Symphony No. 9* (first movement)

Variation No. 6 — Train Robbery
*12 Honegger: *Pacific 231*

Variation No. 9 — The Tribe
*6 Milhaud: Creation of the World

BASIC LIST

(Selections with an asterisk noted in the Workshop Suggestions are on this list.) Wherever specific records represent the best buy because of the number of useful selections contained, record numbers have been supplied.

1. Debussy: *La Mer; Prelude a l'Apres-Midi d'un Faune;*
   Ravel: Daphnis et Chloe Suite No. 2
   Deutsche Grammophon 138923

2. Holst: *The Planets*

3. Dvorak: *Serenade in E for Strings, Op. 22*

4. Tchaikovsky: *Symphony No. 6* (Pathetique)

5. Scarlatti: Sonatas for harpsichord (any collection as long as it is played on the harpsichord)

6. Stravinsky: *L'Histoire du Soldat;* Milhaud: *Creation du Monde*
   Everest 3017

7. Pfeiffer: *Electronomusic*
   Victrola VICS 1371

8. Debussy: *Children's Corner Suite: Claire de Lune; Five Preludes* (piano music)
   Connoisseur S-1866

9. Copland: *Billy the Kid; Rodeo* (usually available on one record)

10. "Meeting at the Summit" (Benny Goodman)
    Gould: *Variations for Clarinet and Band;* Copland: *Concerto for Clarinet and Orchestra;* Stravinsky: *Ebony Concerto:* Bernstein: *Prelude, Fugue and Riffs*
    Columbia MS-6805

11. Schoenberg: *Five Pieces for Orchestra, Op. 16*
    Nonesuch 71192

12. Varese: *Ameriques;* Honegger: *Pacific 231;* Milhaud: *L'Homme et son Desir*
    Vanguard Everyman SRV 274SD

13. "Ports of Call"
    Ravel: *Bolero; La Valse, Pavane;* Ibert: *Escales;* Debussy: *Claire de Lune;* Chabrier: *Espana*
    Columbia MS 6478

14. Partch: *The World of Harry Partch* (playing his own unique musical instruments)
    Columbia MS 7207

15. Subotnick: *Silver Apples of the Moon* (electronic music)
    Nonesuch 71174

16. Takemitsu: *Coral Island; Water Music; Vocalism Ai*
    Victrola VICS-1334

17. Mussorgsky-Ravel: *Pictures at an Exhibition*

EXTENDED LIST

18. Rodrigo: *Concierto de Aranjuez*

19. Prokofiev: *The Stone Flower*

20. J. S. Bach: *Goldberg Variations* (harpsichord version)

21. Spike Jones: any

22. "Electronic Music"
    Music of Avni, Carlos, Mimaroglu, and Lewin-Richter
    Turnabout 34004

23. Prokofiev: *Romeo and Juliet* (Ballet Suite)

24. Subotnick: *Sidewinder* (electronic music)
    Columbia M 30683

25. Tomita: "Snowflakes are Dancing" (electronic performances of ten Debussy tone paintings)
    RCA Arl 1-0488

26. Anderson: *Syncopated Clock* (available in many Anderson collections)

27. Respighi: *Fountains of Rome; Pines of Rome* (often on one record)

28. Stravinsky: *The Rite of Spring*

29. Miles Davis: *Kind of Blue,* Columbia CS-8163
    In a Silent Way, Columbia CS-9875
    Bitches' Brew (2 records), Columbia GP-26

30. Prokofiev: *Alexander Nevsky*

31. Verdi: *March from Aida*
    Try Deutsche Grammophon DG-2530200

32. Rossini: *Overture to William Tell* (obtainable in many overture collections)

33. Mystic Moods Orchestra: "One Stormy Night", "Hiway One", "Awakening" (all available on Warner Bros. label)

34. Environments Disc No. 1: *The Psychologically Ultimate Seashore; Optimum Aviary*
    Atlantic SD 66001

35. Environments Disc No. 2: *Tintinnabulation; Dawn at New Hope, Pennsylvania*
    Atlantic SD 68002

36. Dvorak: *Symphony No. 9* (From the New World)

37. Paul Horn: "Inside II" (flute)
    Epic KE 31600

38. Berlioz: *Roman Carnival* (available in combination with other works by Berlioz)

39. Calliope: (Try Big Top Circus Calliope
    Audio Fidelity Stereodisc AFSD 5986)

40. Pink Floyd: *A Saucerful of Secrets*
    Capitol (EMI) ST 6279

ABOUT THE AUTHOR
Betty C. Keller

Creative writing and drama have been the continuing concerns of Betty C. Keller for the past 20 years. She has taught these subjects at the secondary and college level in several Canadian schools as well as at Numan Women's Teachers' College in Gongola State, northeastern Nigeria.

More than a teacher, Keller is also a playwright, having written several full-length plays in addition to the many drama sketches included in this book.

She has been especially active in drama festival activities, having served as chairperson and co-chairperson at many drama conferences.

Her credentials for a book about drama are excellent, for her ideas are not theory, but a reflection of her experience. The suggestions are practical and do-able because she has walked in the shoes of the drama coaches who are the most probable readers of this book.

ORDER FORM

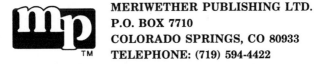

MERIWETHER PUBLISHING LTD.
P.O. BOX 7710
COLORADO SPRINGS, CO 80933
TELEPHONE: (719) 594-4422

Please send me the following books:

_____ **Improvisations in Creative Drama #TT-B138** $12.95
by Betty Keller
A collection of improvisational exercises and sketches for acting students

_____ **Improve With Improv! #TT-B160** $12.95
by Brie Jones
A guide to improvisation and character development

_____ **Theatre Games for Young Performers #TT-B188** $12.95
by Maria C. Novelly
Improvisations and exercises for developing acting skills

_____ **Acting Games — Improvisations and** $12.95
Exercises #TT-B168
by Marsh Cassady
A textbook of theatre games and improvisations

_____ **Truth in Comedy #TT-B164** $12.95
by Charna Halpern, Del Close and Kim "Howard" Johnson
The manual of improvisation

_____ **Winning Monologs for Young Actors #TT-B127** $12.95
by Peg Kehret
Honest-to-life monologs for young actors

_____ **Comedy Improvisation #TT-B175** $12.95
by Delton T. Horn
Improv structures and exercises for actors

**These and other fine Meriwether Publishing books are available
at your local bookstore or direct from the publisher. Use the
handy order form on this page.**

NAME: _____

ORGANIZATION NAME: _____

ADDRESS: _____

CITY:_____ STATE: _____ ZIP: _____

PHONE: _____
  ❏ **Check Enclosed**
  ❏ **Visa or MasterCard #** _____
                                         Expiration
Signature: _____ *Date:* _____
        (required for Visa/MasterCard orders)

COLORADO RESIDENTS: Please add 3% sales tax.
SHIPPING: Include $2.75 for the first book and 50¢ for each additional book ordered.

  ❏ *Please send me a copy of your complete catalog of books and plays.*

ORDER FORM

MERIWETHER PUBLISHING LTD.
P.O. BOX 7710
COLORADO SPRINGS, CO 80933
TELEPHONE: (719) 594-4422

Please send me the following books:

_____ **Improvisations in Creative Drama #TT-B138** $12.95
by Betty Keller
A collection of improvisational exercises and sketches for acting students

_____ **Improve With Improv! #TT-B160** $12.95
by Brie Jones
A guide to improvisation and character development

_____ **Theatre Games for Young Performers #TT-B188** $12.95
by Maria C. Novelly
Improvisations and exercises for developing acting skills

_____ **Acting Games — Improvisations and** $12.95
Exercises #TT-B168
by Marsh Cassady
A textbook of theatre games and improvisations

_____ **Truth in Comedy #TT-B164** $12.95
by Charna Halpern, Del Close and Kim "Howard" Johnson
The manual of improvisation

_____ **Winning Monologs for Young Actors #TT-B127** $12.95
by Peg Kehret
Honest-to-life monologs for young actors

_____ **Comedy Improvisation #TT-B175** $12.95
by Delton T. Horn
Improv structures and exercises for actors

**These and other fine Meriwether Publishing books are available
at your local bookstore or direct from the publisher. Use the
handy order form on this page.**

NAME: _____

ORGANIZATION NAME: _____

ADDRESS: _____

CITY:_____ STATE: _____ ZIP: _____

PHONE: _____

□ **Check Enclosed**
□ **Visa or MasterCard #** _____

Signature: _____ *Expiration Date:* _____

(required for Visa/MasterCard orders)

COLORADO RESIDENTS: Please add 3% sales tax.
SHIPPING: Include $2.75 for the first book and 50¢ for each additional book ordered.

□ *Please send me a copy of your complete catalog of books and plays.*